Induction

This book is dedicated to the millions of children whose lives will be forever touched by the educators we all bring to the classroom each year. They are our inspiration. It is always about the children.

Roberta Richin   Richard Banyon   Rita P. Stein   Francine Banyon

Induction

Connecting Teacher
Recruitment to Retention

Foreword by Harvey J. Stedman, Vice-Chancellor, New York University

CORWIN PRESS, INC.
A Sage Publications Company
Thousand Oaks, California

For information:

Corwin Press, Inc.
A Sage Publications Company
2455 Teller Road
Thousand Oaks, California 91320
www.corwinpress.com

Sage Publications Ltd.
6 Bonhill Street
London EC2A 4PU
United Kingdom

Sage Publications India Pvt. Ltd.
B-42 Panchsheel Enclave
Post Box 4109
New Delhi 110 017 India

Printed in the United States of America

Library of Congress Cataloging-in-Publication Data

Induction: Connecting teacher recruitment to retention / by Roberta Richin … [et al.].
     p.cm.
Includes bibliographical references and index.
ISBN 0-7619-4675-6
ISBN 0-7619-4676-4 (pbk)
   1. Teacher—Recruiting—United States. 2. Teacher turnover—United States—Prevention. 3. Teachers—Selection and appointment—United States. I. Richin, Roberta.
LB2835.25.I53.2003
331.7′6113711′00973—dc21

2002156707

This book is printed on acid-free paper.

03 04 05 06 10 9 8 7 6 5 4 3 2 1

Acquisitions Editor:	Robert D. Clouse
Associate Editor:	Kristen L. Gibson
Editorial Assistant:	Jingle Vea
Copy Editor:	Robert Holm
Production Editor:	Denise Santoyo
Typesetter:	C&M Digitals (P) Ltd.
Indexer:	Pamela Van Huss
Cover Designer:	Michael Dubowe

CONTENTS

List of Tables and Figures

Foreword

A young man leaving his position as a high school English teacher recently completed his exit discussion with his principal. He said he entered the profession after achieving a reasonable level of academic proficiency in the area of language and literature. After teaching for two years, he still felt prepared to teach English but said he was leaving the profession because he did not feel prepared to teach students.

We all know teachers who successfully teach and inspire their students. In addition to their command of a subject matter area, they are generally known by the connections they make with their students and by the fact that they keep learning new ways to help their students achieve. More often than not, their students admire them, consistently learn from them, and feel connected to them years after any formal relationship has ended.

We can all summon up memories of teachers who continue to guide us long after we leave them.

When I left the small town where I grew up and "went to college" at the State University of New York at Fredonia, educators such as Dr. Dawley and Dr. Bernstein inspired me and countless others to love history, learning, and the art of citizenship. There was also the college president, Dr. Langford, whose near physical blindness never prevented him from seeing things and saying things with clarity and kindness, whether he was connecting with an aspiring undergraduate or a senior faculty leader.

As educators accountable for preparing men and women to become and remain accomplished teachers, we must focus our energies on strategies that promote teachers' capabilities to help all children learn well, stay safe, and graduate. At its base, effective teaching involves transforming possibilities into realities. Those who love to teach are able to turn possibility into reality, one child, one school, one community at a time.

It has been my experience that teachers are more likely to help their students learn if the teachers themselves feel they are valued members of a school community that supports and celebrates successful teaching and learning. We can facilitate their success by using the same expertise and optimism we expect them to bring to their students.

This book offers a valuable and practical framework for thinking about how to teach successfully—year after year, class after class, student after student. It contains many insights and lessons from teachers who have found their own professional experiences genuinely rewarding and who did remain in the profession for a lifetime.

—Harvey J. Stedman, Ph.D.
Vice-Chancellor, New York University

Acknowledgments

First, we acknowledge our debt of gratitude to our own teachers, who helped inspire us to become and remain educators. Among them we name Mr. Ignasher, Miss Clarke, Miss Leslie, Mr. Snyder, Mr. Thomas, Mr. Miner, and Mrs. Baker. We are humbled and inspired by their example.

Next, we acknowledge a similar debt of gratitude to those who were our students, colleagues, teachers, and supervisors in the first years of our own professional lives. They helped us establish and sustain the enduring connections that have become our lifelong commitment to schooling. Among these we include Steve DeVito, Stephen Frederico, Louise Frederico, Edward C. Porter, Cecil A. Ramsey, Terry A. Schwartz, Beth Snyder, John Hewlett, Paul McSloy, Harold Saltzman, James Killoran, Margaret Offenberger, Mary Lou Griffin, Stephanie Snyder, Sidney Glassman, John Steinbeck, Eugene O'Neill, Tennessee Williams, and Edward Albee.

To the colleagues who supported our journey to and through this book, we are especially grateful. Their time, wisdom, and comments helped us create the book we intended. Like winners at an awards event, we know any gratitude list will be incomplete. In that light, we still thank Carle Place Superintendent Dr. Patricia Hanson, Half Hollow Hills Superintendent Dr. Sheldon Karnilow, South Country Superintendent Dr. Mark Schissler, Deer Park Superintendent Mr. Don Bright, as well as David Flatley, Bruce Kollmar, Kenneth DellaPorta, Joann Stedman, Vice-Chancellor of New York University Dr. Harvey Stedman, Half Hollow Hills Teacher Association President Richard Lee, and especially Fillmore Peltz and Owen Spanier, Deer Park High School principals. Also, we owe a debt of gratitude to the Deer Park Board of Education and the Carle Place Board of Education.

Since our families and friends survived our first collaboration, they approached this second effort with the advantage that comes from experience. Just as they did the first time around, they provided the countless gestures of love and encouragement that made our continuing collaboration possible. Among them we especially thank Laurette Richin, Irving Richin, Eve Richin, Denise Coleman, Sylvia, Billy and the Tuesday night crowd, Jarrett and Heather Stein, Norell Stein, Justin Young, Barbara and Leonard Zuckerman, Linda and Barry Jacknow, "my honey" Victor, my nieces and nephews, Roberta and Howard Ellen, Nancy and Charlie Erdich, Alexis and Matt Huck, Erica Banyon, Lauren Banyon, Philip Banyon, Dolly and Robert Baratta, Joanne and Gerald Baratta, Margaret and Art Brown, Maggie and Ken Baratta, Marie and Al Andrea, Frank

Sansiveri, Rosanne Pilieri, George Sansiveri, Sherri and Bernard Vishnick, Pat and Colin Campbell, Peggy and Walter Offenberger, Della and Warren Meister, the "Suss," and the family dog, DOS. Our work resonates with Marc Stein's words and thoughts that are always on our minds.

We close this section by gratefully acknowledging those who literally encouraged us through each page of this project: our copy editor, Robert Holm, for his tireless, meticulous attention to the spirit and letter of our work; our editor Dr. Mark Goldberg, for his expertise, guidance, unflagging good humor, and willingness to further aide, abet, and facilitate our collaboration; and our senior editor Robb Clouse, of Corwin Press, for his keen interest, accessibility, and for welcoming us into his publishing community, which is so clearly dedicated to helping schools help children learn well and stay safe.

Also, Corwin Press gratefully acknowledges the contributions of the following reveiwers:

Linda R. Morrow, Ph.D.
Professor
University of Arkansas
Fayetteville, Arkansas

Dr. Marsha Sprague
Professor, Education Department
Christopher Newport University
Newport News, VA

Mary Brooks
Site Coordinator, Beginning Teacher Mentor Program
West Des Moines Community School District
West Des Moines, IA

Bobette Dunn, Ed.D.
Fort Bend ISD
Sugar Land, TX

Dr. Cecilia M. Pierce
UAB School of Education
Birmingham, AL

Dr. Mark M. Jacobs
Supervisor, Attendance & Census
Webster Central School District

About the Authors

Roberta A. Richin is a nationally recognized author and educator specializing in improving student learning and safety through professional development. With Banyon, Banyon, and Stein, Richin is a cofounder of the Connecting Character to Conduct consulting team and coauthor of a book and related materials of the same title. Her model for leadership and consensus building is used by public and private schools, law enforcement organizations, parent-community groups, and corporations. Richin has presented this model at numerous conferences conducted by such organizations as the American Association of School Administrators, Association for Supervision and Curriculum Development, Children's Defense Fund, National Symposium on Child Victimization, School Administrator's Association of New York State, New York State Education Department Conference on Inclusive Schools and Communities, the Nassau-Suffolk Bar Association, the Center for Prejudice Reduction, and the Parent-Teacher Association. Since 1975, Richin has published journal articles and curricula and has contributed to books focusing on the education and well-being of children and families. Richin continues to dedicate the majority of her time to providing school-based support for instruction by collaborating with students, teachers, administrators, and parents at the classroom, building, district, community, and university levels. She and her colleagues can be reached at inductionhelp@aol.com.

Richard Banyon is presently consulting in the Carle Place, New York, school district as Assistant Superintendent for Curriculum, Instruction and Personnel. His educational career spans over 35 years as a classroom teacher, guidance counselor, dean, building administrator, and central office administrator in New York City and Long Island. He most recently was Assistant Superintendent for Personnel, Curriculum, and Instruction for the Deer Park School District, where he piloted a fully integrated model of induction specifically focused on recruiting and retaining teachers and administrators. He has facilitated national and regional workshops and conducted job-embedded professional development on such issues as supervision, observation, evaluation, and preparing new teachers for the classroom. With Banyon, Stein, and Richin he is a cofounder of the Connecting Character to Conduct consulting team and coauthor of a book of the same title.

Rita Prager Stein has been a central office administrator involved in curriculum, recruitment, and retention for more than twenty years. During this time, she has recruited, hired, and retained more than ten thousand employees. She has spoken on recruitment and retention at the Association of School Personnel Administrators, as well as other national conferences including the New England Middle Schools, Association for Supervision and Curriculum Development (ASCD), and Phi Delta Kappa. Stein is a coauthor of the ASCD book *Connecting Character to Conduct: Helping Students Do the Right Things* (2000). Her work on supervision and evaluation has been reviewed and utilized by several school districts throughout New York State. She has appeared on several television shows including *Tools for Schools*, a show on professional development and character, as well as on many radio broadcasts. Her doctoral dissertation focused on the effect of instruction on the moral reasoning of students. She has presented workshops on this topic at Columbia University and New York University, as well as districts throughout Long Island, Pennsylvania, and New Jersey. She has presented workshops in New Orleans, Providence, Dallas, Boston, and at several prestigious conferences. She is an adjunct professor at the State University of New York at Stony Brook and, with Roberta Richin, has published in the New England Middle School Journal. She can be reached at drritastein@aol.com.

Francine Banyon has 35 years of experience as an educator in New York City schools, the Huntington School District, and the Smithtown Central School District on Long Island. With Richin, Banyon and Stein, Banyon is cofounder of the Connecting Character to Conduct consulting team and a coauthor of a book of the same title. She has been the team leader in a New York State model dropout prevention program, a dean, a building administrator, and mentor to numerous present administrators working in Long Island school districts. Banyon has worked with teams to create student internship programs, Renaissance student success programs, conflict resolution-mediation programs, and school-to-business partnerships, all of which have continued to grow after her departure. As an educational consultant Banyon has presented at numerous workshops throughout the United States and has conducted extensive job-embedded professional development for instructional, administrative, and support staff in public and private schools.

Introduction

Induction—From Recruitment to Retention

This book is designed to help all of the administrators, teachers, and board of education members who will participate in the hiring of more than 2 million new teachers between now and 2015. Representing the replacement of more than 70 percent of the professional staff currently employed, this is the largest replacement effort ever undertaken in American schools. Factors contributing to that high number include

- Class size reduction policies
- Enrollment growth
- Retirements
- Teachers leaving after two to five years
- Diversity issues
- New learning standards, assessments, graduation requirements and student needs, all combining to create new demands for teachers in particular certification areas

If you expect to hire several teachers or more over the next years, this book will help you. The gap between supply of and demand for qualified professional staff can make recruiting and retaining all types of candidates extremely competitive. Perhaps you anticipate fewer new teachers than others. Be aware that the competitive climate can make it difficult to recruit even a small number of teachers and even more difficult to keep those you have already recruited. This book is designed to help you with every aspect of the recruitment and retention process.

Traditional networking, advertising, reassigning existing staff, and offering promotions to fill gaps can leave your school unprepared to meet new learning and safety goals typically itemized on today's school report cards, in mission statements, or in local standards. The educators you hire will prepare children to meet rigorous and often changing state standards, to achieve on assessments, and to prepare for college or vocational training where the demands change more rapidly than ever. Recruiting educators is not just a matter of filling vacancies. It is a matter of shaping the future one professional, one child, one school community at a time.

Each time you sign a contract with an educator, you are choosing someone responsible for helping children learn well and stay safe. Therefore, recruitment and retention form the foundation for achieving your school community's learning and safety goals. Your student achievement and school safety record are directly related to the instructional skills and practices of your professional staff (see Educational Testing Service [2000], *How Teaching Matters: Bringing the Classroom Back to Discussions of Teacher Quality*). Given the importance of every decision you make to hire or permanently retain an educator, you can benefit from building on a strong foundation of proven practices. That foundation is composed of five interlocking "building blocks" we have been using and refining to meet our evolving staffing goals over the past thirty-five years.

These five Building Blocks are an organizing framework you can use to help one teacher or dozens of teachers in your school or district complete their three-year process from recruitment to tenure or job stability. We devote a chapter to each Building Block because each is an essential element of a comprehensive recruitment and retention program. Decision makers frequently select or adapt different elements from each block to meet their own school community goals.

As you explore the options offered in each Building Block, you can create a custom approach to recruitment and retention that will meet your school's individual learning and safety goals now and for years to come. While we refer to our system as a "BluePrint," we understand that it is a blueprint that should be modified to fit the demographics and special needs of your situation.

BUILDING BLOCK 1: PREPARING

- Recognizing your induction needs
- Developing your mission statement
- Establishing your policy on induction
- Setting your board of education induction goal(s)

BUILDING BLOCK 2: STAFFING

- Recruiting
- Interviewing
- Hiring

BUILDING BLOCK 3: ORIENTING: YEAR ONE

- Starting before the first school year begins
- Conducting professional development
- Mentoring and collaborating
- Supervising, observing, and evaluating

BUILDING BLOCK 4: CONNECTING: YEARS TWO AND THREE

- Continuing professional development
- Supervising, observing, and evaluating
- Granting tenure/permanence

BUILDING BLOCK 5: RETAINING YOUR STAFF

- Sustaining the connection
- Supervising, observing, and evaluating: Developing career-long learners
- Renewing and reorienting

As you will discover in each chapter, we use the example of the "Centerville" school community to illustrate how your district or school can choose and use best practices for attracting and keeping educators. The "Centerville" school community is a composite of the best practices in about twenty schools we've worked in and with over the past thirty-five years. The Centerville school culture is dedicated to promoting serious learning and safety in every aspect of schooling. The district approaches induction as a means of achieving its learning and safety goals. In this fashion, the district fulfills its mission.

You will see how the members of the Centerville recruitment staff use each of the five Building Blocks to construct a practical plan to recruit and retain staff. We invite you to join the Centerville team by following along and constructing your own BluePrint. For example, you will see how the Centerville team uses Building Block 1 to begin its induction plan by reviewing their related policies, procedures, and staffing needs. Their efforts produce a solid foundation for Building Block 2, where the team completes each phase of induction activities over three years.

During that three-year journey "from recruitment to retention," the Centerville team uses Building Block 3 to retain their newly recruited staff by connecting with each new recruit through supervision, observation, evaluation, and professional development activities. Through Building Blocks 3, 4, and 5, you will discover how the Centerville induction plan balances staffing change and continuity by creating opportunities for new and veteran staff to get to know each other, develop supportive relationships, and build new traditions.

Each chapter includes many practical examples illustrating how administrators, teachers, other school community members, and the newly hired professionals fulfill their roles in the induction process. Special highlights demonstrate how Centerville uses each of the interlocking Building Blocks to create a professional culture where staff members meet student needs by using best professional practices throughout their careers. You will see many examples of how this professional culture is part of the over-all plan to retain the most qualified staff.

In Building Block 4, you will follow Centerville's culminating activities as the board of education, administration, and candidates for tenure/permanence complete their journey from recruitment to the early stages of retention. These activities are opportunities to recognize teachers for meeting or exceeding goals at each benchmark of their journey from recruitment to tenure/permanent employment.

As you complete Building Block 5, you will discover how you can use the principles of orientation and connection to continually renew and energize your entire staff.

■ CHOOSING AND USING SUCCESSFUL PRACTICES

If you are responsible for helping to recruit or retain staff, you know what it feels like to ask yourself, "How will this professional fulfill his or her role in five years? Ten? Twenty years or more?" This book helps you ask the right questions and find the right answers for your individual school community. We have organized this book so your induction plan meets your school community's goals and needs. Since you know your school community's unique strengths, challenges, and other characteristics, this book allows you to choose from a wide variety of proven practices you can use to attract and retain the best professional staff in this competitive market.

Each chapter ends with two special sections: "Tips" and "BluePrint" for that special Building Block.

BluePrint

You can use the BluePrint (Resource A) to choose and use the best practices for your school or district. You will notice that the BluePrint in Resource A puts all five Building Blocks together in a way that gives you an instant overview of a comprehensive induction program. In addition, you will find that each chapter features the elements of the BluePrint that relate to that Building Block. For example, Chapter 1 closes with the section of the BluePrint dedicated to Building Block 1: Preparing. Chapter 2 closes with the section of the BluePrint dedicated to Building Block 2: Staffing, and so on.

Tips

In the Tips section of each chapter, you will find additional practices and strategies you may use to achieve your induction goals. We have often used these strategies to help districts and schools achieve their goals. These tips are organized into the following six categories that directly impact on induction:

Connections

Connections include:

- Leadership practices that promote a strong sense of shared purpose. "Leadership is the exercise of wit and will, principle and passion, time and talent, and purpose and power in a way that allows the group to increase the likelihood that shared goals will be accomplished."[1]

- Strategies and activities that promote communication and understanding between and among stakeholder groups, including parents, community groups, and so forth
- Characteristics of the school community that motivate people to join the district and remain with the district

Data Mining

- Data mining includes strategies and activities for gathering, analyzing, reporting, and otherwise using information to make the right decisions.

Finance

- Finances involve variables related to the district budget.

Legal Issues

- Legal issues include variables related to federal, state, local, and other laws, statutes and/or policies.

Personnel Issues

- Personnel issues relate to staffing and human resources.

Professional Development

- Professional development encompasses the full range of formal and informal strategies and activities that helps members of the faculty and staff use best practices to advance student achievement and school safety.

As you follow the members of the Centerville school community as they use the suggested strategies and activities, consider how their induction practices stabilize their school community and support student performance during periods of significant change in leadership and instructional staff.

SUMMARY ■

Professional journals and popular media are already warning that trends in recruitment, retirement, teachers leaving the system prematurely, and increasing enrollments will produce teacher shortages that will leave our schools unprepared to help all our children meet or exceed new standards and assessments. When we conduct professional development activities, people who share your responsibilities for induction raise such questions as the following:

- "What strategies can we use to find the best teacher candidates for our students?"
- "What will motivate the best teachers to join our staff?"
- "Once teachers join our staff, how can we keep them with us, even when other places may seem equally attractive in some ways?"

- "How can we attract and keep the best teachers for all our students, especially in difficult-to-staff areas over a period of years?"
- "How can we help our staff, our students, and our parents maintain connections to each other during the induction process?"

You will discover answers to these and other key questions in each of the five interlocking Building Blocks in this book. As you explore the options offered in each Building Block, you can create a custom approach to induction that will meet your school's learning and safety goals now and for years to come.

■ **NOTE**

1. Sergiovanni, T. (1994). *Building community in schools.* San Francisco: Jossey-Bass, 170.

1

Preparing to Recruit and Retain

THIS CHAPTER WILL HELP YOU

- Prepare for your induction initiative
- Clarify leadership roles in your induction initiative
- Connect induction to your school goals
- Establish induction goals

As Personnel Director Stephanie Blair walked into the welcome-back breakfast on the first day of school, she joined board of education President Andrew Koller on the coffee line. President Koller congratulated Stephanie on the Task Force on Induction's success on the board goal he had championed for the past three years.

"This assembly program is the culmination of the past three years of the induction initiative, Stephanie. These newly tenured educators are the first to have completed every Building Block of our initiative."

"Thank you, Andrew. We could not have accomplished the goals you set without the strong support and leadership of the board of education. . . . And we've only just begun!"

As the personnel director finished her coffee and made her way to the front of the auditorium, she recalled the cabinet meetings more than three years ago when she first presented information supporting her concerns regarding attracting and retaining quality educators at Centerville. This was a new problem for the Centerville schools. Previously staffing focused on replacing educators who were retiring at a rate that matched the availability of individuals qualified to replace them. Now the rate of retirement was greater than the existing pool of qualified applicants, new certifications were in demand, and some valued teachers were leaving to take positions in other districts—often as administrators—and even in the business world. She reflected on how the district used a three-step process to prepare for recruiting and retaining qualified educators:

1. The personnel director shared information with the superintendent.
2. The superintendent used the information to prepare and share a report with the board of education.
3. The superintendent, board of education, and personnel director collaboratively used the district decision-making framework to ensure that
   a. All efforts advanced the district mission and shared purpose;
   b. District policy was articulated;
   c. District goals were set;
   d. Objectives were identified;
   e. Roles of leaders were articulated in relation to the goals.

During step 1 and 2 of the "preparation process," the superintendent used the information the personnel director shared to prepare a report to the board of education regarding new personnel issues. He emphasized the past patterns of retirements, resignations, and recruitment efforts. During the board of education work sessions over the next few months, the superintendent and the personnel director engaged the members of the board of education in substantive, data-driven discussions. The board learned what the staffing needs would be for the following year as well as for the subsequent four years. Based on past patterns and the ages of senior staff members, the board saw what openings would occur in the next five years as a result of staff members, primarily teachers, retiring, leaving the profession or moving into administrative positions in this or other districts.

During step 3 of the "preparation process," the board of education convened to set goals for the upcoming school year. To prepare for setting the goals, they agreed on one objective and made one essential commitment. The objective was to revise the board of education policy on induction/ staffing (Figure 1.3). The commitment was to provide the human and financial resources necessary to achieve the goals they set.

The superintendent began a board of education work session dedicated to revising the board goals by reviewing the district mission statement as the context for all Centerville policies and practices.[1]

In collaboration with the superintendent, the members of the board of education used a framework called "F.O.C.U.S." to help each other connect

Figure 1.1　Centerville School District Mission Statement

Centerville School District Mission Statement

The mission of the Centerville School District is to help
all our children learn well, stay safe, and graduate as
contributing members of our global community. We are
dedicated to providing the resources and opportunities
that will help our staff and students excel in our increasingly
challenging, continuously changing society. We shall fulfill this
mission in full partnership with the parents and other
stakeholders of our Centerville community.

the mission statement (see Figure 1.1) to the induction policies they set and the procedures they would follow to set their goals.

Find/create
Opportunities to
Connect recruitment to retention
Using
Standards of induction

The superintendent and members of the board of education used their "Framework for Decision Making" (Figure 1.2) throughout their work session.

Using the Framework for Decision Making, the board of education adopted Goal 1:

Goal 1	*Objectives*	*Timeline*	*Lead Staff Member*
To attract and retain qualified educators.	Create a comprehensive induction policy that attracts and retains the best qualified educators to Centerville School District.	First month of school year	personnel director
	Provide the resources to achieve this goal.	Through the budget process and subsequent adoption	superintendent

Figure 1.2 Centerville School District Framework for Decision Making

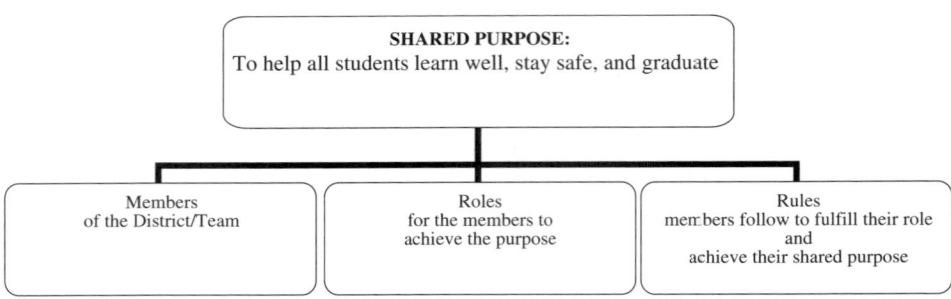

Based on their induction-related objective, commitment, and goal, the board of education adopted, the policy on induction shown in Figure 1.3.

After the board of education adopted all the induction goals, objectives and policies, the superintendent charged the personnel director with the responsibility of implementing the induction goal: To attract and retain qualified educators.

It had been just over three years since the personnel director began to implement that charge. At the time, the task seemed overwhelming, so she created a task force of stakeholders to help her achieve the induction goal set by the board of education. The members of the Centerville Task Force included professional educators and members of the community. They were selected on the basis of the following criteria:

- Their expertise in the area of recruitment and retention
- Their "people-skills" in the areas of collaborating to achieve shared goals in specific time frames
- Their knowledge of the district, the students, and the characteristics of "quality" educators (those who presented the greatest mastery of instructional delivery, classroom management, knowledge of student characteristics, and commitment to career-long learning).

The district used somewhat different procedures to select the administrators, teachers, and community members, respectively. Administrators were selected by the superintendent. Teachers were selected through a collaborative process involving their principals and their teacher association. Community members were selected through the same process the district used to select the community members of the shared decision-making and site-based management teams. The parent/community member was selected by the parent association, and the at-large community member was selected by the members of the local civic association. The Centerville Task Force was composed of nine members:

- Two central office administrators
- Two principals
- Three teachers
- Two community members

Figure 1.3　Centerville School District Policy on Induction

The Centerville School District recognizes that the district needs to replace retiring educators, attract appropriately certified new educators, and retain the best qualified educators to meet the needs of all students.

Therefore, the Centerville School District will create procedures to implement and evaluate a comprehensive induction initiative that will ensure that our district:

- Attracts the best-qualified educators to the Centerville School District
- Hires the best-qualified educators
- Retains the best-qualified educators

The first thing Centerville Task Force members did as a team was to

- Become familiar with the data the district used to create the board policy and set board goals regarding recruiting and retaining quality educators;
- Review and explore best practices for recruiting and retaining professional staff.

As a result of that initial data mining, they adopted the Induction: Connecting Recruitment to Retention approach. They were now in position to move to Building Block 2: Staffing, the absolutely crucial steps involved in recruiting, interviewing, and hiring new staff.

CHAPTER SUMMARY ■

This chapter was designed to help you accomplish four goals. First, it provided an organizing framework you can use to prepare for induction. Second, it defined criteria to consider in formulating induction-related roles for the members of your leadership team. Third, it established the importance of connecting your induction initiative to your other district goals. Fourth, it clarified how your induction initiative will attract and retain the right personnel when aligned with your school or district goals.

Tips

DISTRICTS AND SCHOOLS OFTEN USE THE FOLLOWING PRACTICES TO PREPARE FOR THEIR INDUCTION INITIATIVE:

Connections

- Prominently post board of education goals in administrative offices, teachers' workrooms, in the school newsletter, on the district website, and so forth.

- Include major stakeholders on your district or school induction task force. If there are specific organizations that should be included because of their central role in advancing student learning, safety, and graduation, you may include them, too.

Data Mining

- Maintain and use careful, updated, and accurate records in all areas of staffing so decisions can be made in a timely and productive fashion.

Finance

- Ensure that the budget reflects the board of education's commitment to supporting the induction goal through human and financial resources.

Legal Issues

- Make sure your induction goals, practices, and preparation activities are consistent with your contract or work rules.

Personnel Issues

- (Also related to **Data Mining**) Set quarterly benchmarks to report updated staffing-related information to relevant stakeholders, including but not limited to the superintendent and members of both the board of education and the induction task force.

Professional Development

- Involve the board of education in a workshop regarding board roles, responsibilities, and other issues related to induction.

■ NOTE

1. Nadeau, A., & Leighton, M. (1996, July). *The role of leadership in sustaining school reform: Voices from the field*. Washington, DC: U.S. Department of Education.

BLUEPRINT FOR BUILDING BLOCK 1

Building Block 1	GOALS	PARTICIPANTS	OBJECTIVES	NEXT STEPS
	Preparing			
__1a	Cabinet meeting on staffing	• Superintendent • Other lead administrators	Reach consensus regarding how to cope with the following issues in a way that is aligned with the district mission statement (see Figure 1.1). • Increasing numbers of retirements • Resignations of relatively new staff • New certifications needed to meet federal/state mandates and local goals/needs.	Superintendent presents to the board of education regarding the need for a more responsive induction policy
__1b	Board of Education: • Adopts a comprehensive induction policy • Incorporates the hiring policy into the induction policy • Sets a board goal regarding Induction: Connecting Recruitment to Retention	Board of Education Leadership Team: • Superintendent • Personnel Director	Superintendent and Cabinet begin to implement the induction policy	• Leadership Team implements district policy by adopting the Induction: Connecting Recruitment to Retention (I:CRR) approach • Members of the Leadership Team organize the district Induction Task Force

(Continued)

BLUEPRINT FOR BUILDING BLOCK 1 *(Continued)*

	GOALS	PARTICIPANTS	OBJECTIVES	NEXT STEPS
__ 1c	Induction Task Force convenes to create a framework matching Figure 1.2 (Induction Framework)	• Superintendent • Board member • Personnel director • Building principals • Teachers Association • Chairpersons • Parent/community member	Establish (up to four) committees on Building Blocks of Induction: • Building Block 2: Staffing • Building Block 3: Orienting • Building Block 4: Connecting • Building Block 5: Retaining	Induction Task Force schedules workshops so all appropriate task force and other committee members learn the induction process
__ 1d	Workshops are convened	Members: • Induction Task Force committee members	Two-day Induction: Connecting Recruitment to Retention workshop: • Topic 1: Team-Building • Topic 2: Using the Induction: Connecting Recruitment to Retention approach with BluePrint	• Evaluate the workshop process • Use the outcomes of the workshop evaluation to provide additional task force and committee training, as needed • Report progress to the superintendent
__ 1e	Establish a three-year induction plan to recruit and retain the best educators	Members: • Induction Task Force • Members of other committees	• Building Block committees use district data to draft a calendar for implementing "appropriate" elements of each Building Block (2 through 5) • Each committee creates a report to the Induction Task Force indicating status of each Building Block • Publicize outcomes, Building Block 1	Initiate all appropriate elements of each Building Block: 2–5

See Appendix A for the Complete BluePrint for all five Building Blocks to Induction

2

Staffing Your School or District

Necessary Tools

THIS CHAPTER WILL HELP YOU

- Use team-building strategies
- Implement your staffing process
- Select recruitment strategies
- Use interviewing techniques
- Hire the best-qualified staff

It was 10:00 a.m., and all the staff members had finally taken their seats to listen to Centerville Superintendent James Frasier kick off the new school year with his annual address. As was tradition, he opened by acknowledging the dedication of his veteran staff, recognizing his newly tenured staff, and welcoming the new members of the district's growing professional community.

This was the first group of newly tenured staff to have completed Centerville's three-year induction journey from recruitment to retention. Personnel Director Stephanie Blair smiled as the veterans and new teachers applauded those who had just been granted tenure.

Stephanie glanced over to high school Principal Owen Spitzer, who was such a crucial member of the induction initiative, and gave him a big thumbs up. "It's all coming together now," she thought as she left the auditorium. Now she felt ready to chair the next task force meeting, where the members would share highlights illustrating how the district incorporated each of the elements of "Building Block 1: Staffing" into their induction initiative. With the information from that meeting, she would complete the first part of her report on "Induction: Connecting Recruitment to Retention" for the superintendent.

■ PUTTING IT TOGETHER

It was easy for the personnel director to focus all the members of the task force on their progress to date. "Okay, everyone, just take a few minutes to review our agenda and scan your copies of the BluePrint. (See Resource A.) As we've discussed, the BluePrint outlines the district's long-term plan for Induction: Connecting Recruitment to Retention. It details our three-year induction plan. We can use it as a handy outline for monitoring our progress."

"Just to remind you, our goal for this meeting is to share highlights of how we have implemented Building Block 2 over the last three years. Over those three years we have phased in each of the five building blocks. We have literally 'built' our staff by linking our staffing, orienting, connecting, and retaining practices."

The personnel director posted the agenda for their session.

As a task force member at the meeting, the elementary school principal who chaired the interviewing subcommittee observed: "This will be easy to put together. The template basically completed itself. All we have to do is fill in the details by sharing the highlights we think have been the most important to our success."

While the members of the three subcommittees (Resource J and Figure 2.2) started to review their respective portions of the "BluePrint for Induction," the personnel director focused on highlighting key aspects of the initial task force team-building activities.

She began by reviewing her first entries in the BluePrint for Induction from their critical staffing meeting just three years ago. *How could they meet their changing staffing needs when it had become so difficult to attract good teachers, much less retain them?*

During that very first meeting, they discussed how Centerville had used the same staff recruitment and retention practices for many years. Their approach was no longer meeting their needs. Like school districts around the country, Centerville had been finding it increasingly difficult to attract and retain the highly trained, dedicated staff to:

- Achieve local curriculum, instruction, assessment, and demographics-related goals and needs

Figure 2.1 Agenda for Task Force Meeting on Building Block 2: Staffing

Our Goals for This Meeting:
A. To Collaboratively Contribute to Centerville's Report on Induction:
  Connecting Recruitment to Retention
B. To Share Highlights of Each of the Three Elements of Staffing: Recruiting,
  Interviewing, and Hiring		

TIME	TOPIC	PRESENTER

10:30 a.m.	Welcome
	Coffee
	Quick focus on board
	  goal for induction
	Quick overview of the
	  workshop agenda
		Superintendent
		Personnel Director and
		Task Force Chair

10:45–11:00	Team building: Using the
	  "Connecting Character to
	  Conduct Approach"
		Personnel Director

11:00–11:30	How to Recruit	Middle School Principal and Cochair, How to Recruit Subcommittee Parent/Community Member and Cochair, How to Recruit Subcommittee
11:30–12:00 p.m.	How to Interview	Elementary School Principal and Chair of How to Interview Subcommittee Teacher and Member of How to Interview Subcommittee
12:00–12:30	Lunch	
12:30–1:00	How to Hire	High School Principal and Chair of the How to Hire Subcommittee

1:00–1:15	Next Steps:
	  Reporting on Building
	  Blocks 2, 3, 4, and 5
		Personnel Director

- Comply with rigorous national and state learning standards, tests, and safety requirements
- Meet federal and state laws and mandates
- Conform to budgetary and other fiscal restraints
- Remain in the district for at least six years

Figure 2.2 Organizational Chart of The Task Force

Organizational Chart of the Task Force

Superintendent Frasier

Induction: Connecting Recruitment to Retention Task Force
Chairperson: Stephanie Blair, Personnel Director

Building Block 1: Preparing

Building Block 2: Staffing

Building Block 3: Orienting

Building Block 4: Connecting

Building Block 5: Retaining

Staffing Subcommittee A: How to Recruit
Co-Chairpersons
Mr. Chuck Bevin, parent, and Middle School Principal Henry F. Rutledge

Staffing Subcommittee B: How to Interview
Chairperson
Elementary School Principal Meredith Griffin; Role of the subcommittee is to set boundaries, standards, basic questions, etc.

Staffing Subcommittee C: How to Hire
Chairperson
High School Principal Owen Spitzer

Interview Committees
- One member of Subcommittee B: "How to Interview"
- Principal
- Department Chair
- Teachers
- Parent(s)

These committee members use resources such as Figure 2.8 to:
1. Interview selected candidates
2. Evaluate the candidates
3. Recommend best candidates to teach a demonstration lesson

Demonstration Lesson Evaluators
- Principal
- Chair
- Teacher(s)

These evaluators use such resources as Figure 2.9 to:
- Receive the name(s) of candidate(s) recommended by the Interview Committee
- Observe candidates teaching the lesson
- Evaluate the demonstration lesson
- Share the evaluations with the Interview Committee

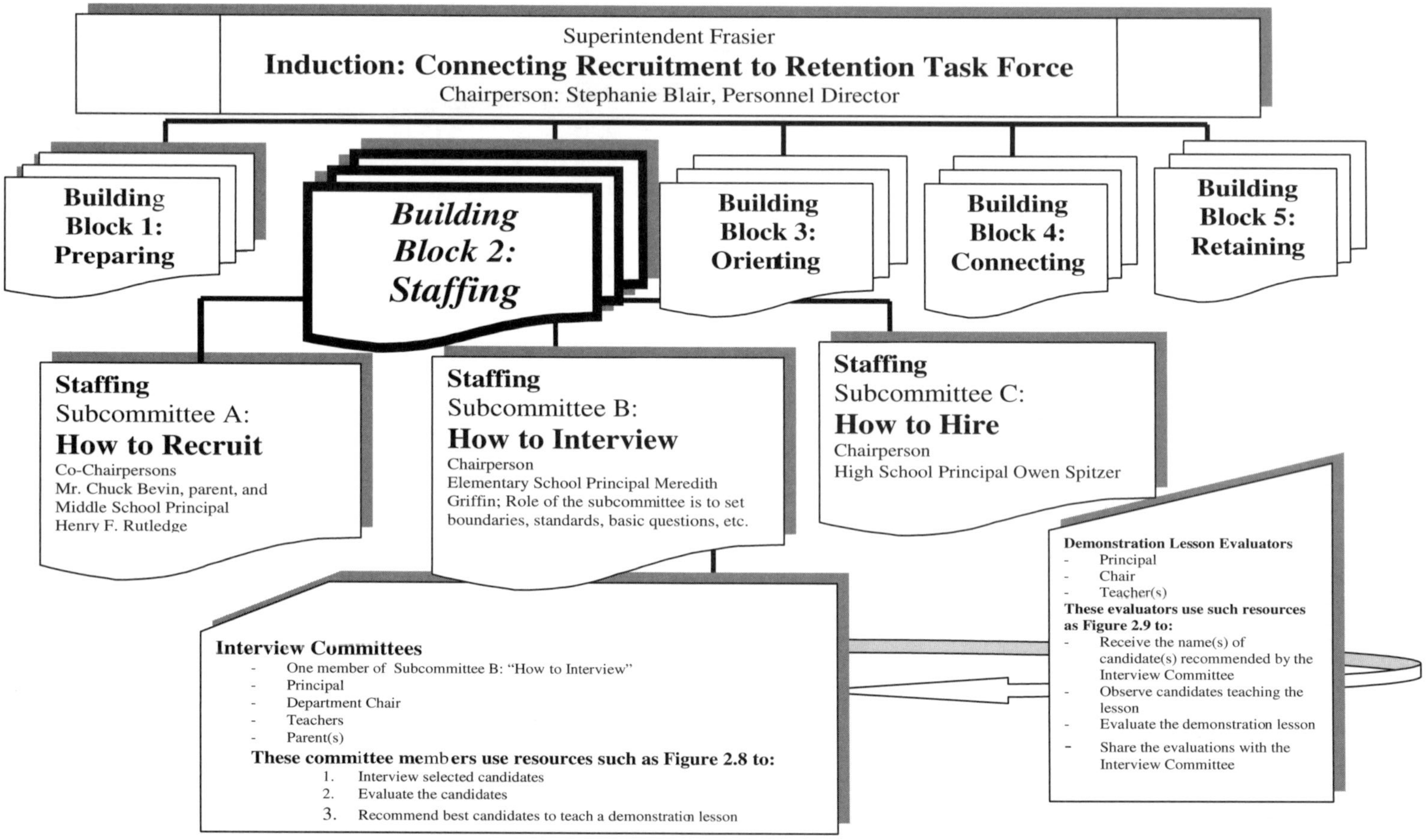

GETTING STARTED   ■

Highlighting Team–Building
Sessions for All Members of the Task
Force on Induction and Related Subcommittees

For so many years, each administrator or supervisor in the room had approached staffing only from his or her own departmental or building-level needs. This was the first time a task force had been convened

- To see staffing as part of the whole induction and retention process
- To see induction from a districtwide perspective

The personnel director and the I-CRR (Induction: Connecting Recruitment to Retention) facilitator planned this first meeting to focus on team building and goal setting. The initial meeting was the first time Centerville's principals, department chairs, teachers, and other leaders agreed to work as a team to achieve an induction-related charge established by the superintendent and the board of education: To create an induction initiative that would help Centerville achieve its learning and safety goals.[1]

The personnel director introduced the induction facilitator for the first meeting of Centerville's task force. The facilitator explained that they would accomplish two main goals by the end of the session.

1. Goal 1: To establish as a team, with a shared purpose, specific and clear roles for members, and a specific set of rules and procedures
2. Goal 2: To agree on steps Centerville will follow to achieve induction goals by connecting recruitment to retention using the Building Blocks: Preparing, Staffing, Orienting, Connecting, and Retaining

When the facilitator said, "Raise your hand if you've ever been a member of a very rewarding and productive team, theatre production, class, or other kind of group," almost every hand went up. "Now raise your hand if you have ever been a member of a frustrating, disappointing team, theatre production, class, or other kind of group!" This time every hand went up, to a chorus of laughter.

The facilitator continued, "Let's brainstorm and compare key characteristics of successful and unsuccessful 'team' experiences we've had, so we can make sure that being a member of this team is rewarding and productive."

The elementary school principal's response captured the sentiments raised across the group: "I can say one thing for sure. My successful team experiences have made me feel connected—belonging—into the project—being part of something bigger than myself. I even loved going to the meetings!"

A middle school social studies teacher offered her best description of the opposite experience. "My unsuccessful team experiences have been the exact opposite. I felt I was responsible for all the work, carrying the load, isolated, unproductive—like nothing was getting done. . . . I hated going to the meetings." They wanted to derive the satisfaction from a "high-challenge,

Figure 2.3 List of Practices of a Successful Team

How Members of the Team Behave as a Team	How Members of the Team Communicate as a Team	How Members of the Team Feel as a Team and as Individuals
■ Seek agreement	■ "Help me understand"	■ Belonging
■ Use respect, impulse control, compassion, and equity (See Figure 1.2)	■ "Can we agree . . .?"	■ Valued
■ Remain focused on their charge	■ "How can I/we help?"	■ Visible
■ Follow directions	■ "Let's try it this way . . ."	■ A sense of accomplishment and progress
■ Help each other	■ "How can we do this a different way?"	■ Purposeful
■ Listen for understanding	■ Using "para-verbals"— Nodding heads, saying "Mmm-hmmm . . ."	■ Respected
■ Encourage a free exchange of differing views	■ Affirm, normalize, refocus (See Resource C)	■ Part of the group process
■ Eye contact	■ Take and maintain accurate minutes	■ Engaged

Note: School districts may wish to create their own list or adapt this one to match their own core values and priorities.

high-skill situation (requiring) concentration and creativity."[2] The group nodded in agreement as they shared a simple list describing the practices of a successful small group or team and agreed to use those practices to achieve their shared and individual induction goals.

The personnel director highlighted the following statement of agreement at the end of the day. "The task force will make all its decisions about induction to advance the larger purposes of Team Centerville." More specifically:

We are the members of the Centerville School District system.

- Systems always have a shared purpose. Our task force shares in Centerville's purpose: to help all children learn well and stay safe. Candidates must fit the needs of a specific school as well as the criteria for success in the district.
- We agree to advance the same purpose, connect to the same members, fulfill our specific roles on our team, and follow the same

rules/procedures that guide all of the Centerville School District activities.[3]

There is an *I* in *TEAM*—the *I* in *TEAM* stands for implied!

- "Remember, if I'm a member of our team, I need to be participate fully!"

We share a common vocabulary.

- We all use the same words to mean the same things at meetings and elsewhere. We discuss what is not clear.

We protect the privacy and confidentiality of every applicant, every committee or subcommittee member involved in the entire induction process, from recruitment to retention.

The personnel director completed her review of the team-building meetings that took place a little over three years ago, and she turned to the parent/community member who was the cochair of the How to Recruit Subcommittee.

"Thanks for giving me the opportunity to give our part of this report," the parent said. "Participating on this subcommittee has given me a new perspective on the budgetary factors involved in attracting the best teachers to our district. I've learned that we can make fiscally responsible decisions and still hire staff who help us achieve our learning and safety goals. Now I understand the budget and just how new staff need to fit into the dollars available. And you can ask the other members! They're more likely to raise the financial issues before I even mention them these days!"

HOW TO RECRUIT

The subcommittee cochair, the middle school principal, continued the report on how to recruit by relating how their group used the anticipated staffing needs document that the building principals and department chairs had submitted to the personnel director. Working with the principals and chairpersons, the personnel director developed a staffing report for all staff in the following categories: full-time, part-time, shared between or among schools, and long-term and short-term leave replacements. Of course, some of these categories overlapped and a chart was developed to show grades, schools and types of positions.

The middle school principal continued, "We used that staffing report to help us create a recruitment plan, which included four components:

Outreach

Advertisement

Public relations

Career ladders"

"In each of these components, we had to focus on the best places to recruit particular staff members based on the data from the staffing report."

"We reviewed Centerville's former recruitment practices in these four areas, and we explored best practices suggested in the I-CRR training. As a result of that process, we discovered that recruiting is not as simple as placing one advertisement in the newspaper or reaching out to a few people we know from colleges."

The middle school French teacher continued with the subcommittee report using the "How to Recruit" section of BluePrint for Induction.

"As you can see, we discovered that recruitment actually involves four interconnected components."

Outreach Highlights

Task Force members teamed with other members of the school community to represent Centerville's staffing and recruitment interests at various local, regional and national job fairs, conferences, colleges and universities, and any other forum that seemed promising. They followed a three-step communications process created at the task force level to make sure that they shared, gathered, stored, and presented information completely and accurately.

The first step of the communications process was simply to build and maintain a web presence. The second step was to ensure that all members of the task force were linked to the web page, received updates through e-mail, and could communicate with each other easily. This web page was also linked to a variety of other schools and organizations involved in preparing and placing educators. The third step was to appoint two task force members to provide updated information to the webmaster, and to communicate appropriately with local, regional and national job fairs, schools of higher education, and other potential resources.

Outreach Highlight 1: Diversity Recruitment Fair

A task force member and the director of guidance brought the directors of secondary science and elementary instruction with her to her alma mater's diversity recruitment fair held near the state capitol. Centerville, like many other districts around the nation, is following a plan to create a more diverse staff from a wider geographic range. Instead of following the traditional approach, in which representatives of the school would distribute information and applications and collect resumes, they approached this fair with special invitations in hand (see Figure 2.5, Special Invitation). The team used a simple three-tiered outreach approach.

1. The team handed out information and accepted applications and resumes, just as they would at any fair.
2. The team reviewed those applications as soon as possible during the recruitment fair.
3. On the basis of those applications, the team's members invited potential recruits to complete a "preliminary interview."

At that point, the on-site contact was completed. If the preliminary interview was promising, Centerville's personnel department would invite that candidate to visit the school community again through the new "Getting to Know You" program. This program was designed especially to

Figure 2.4 The Four Interconnected Components of "How to Recruit"

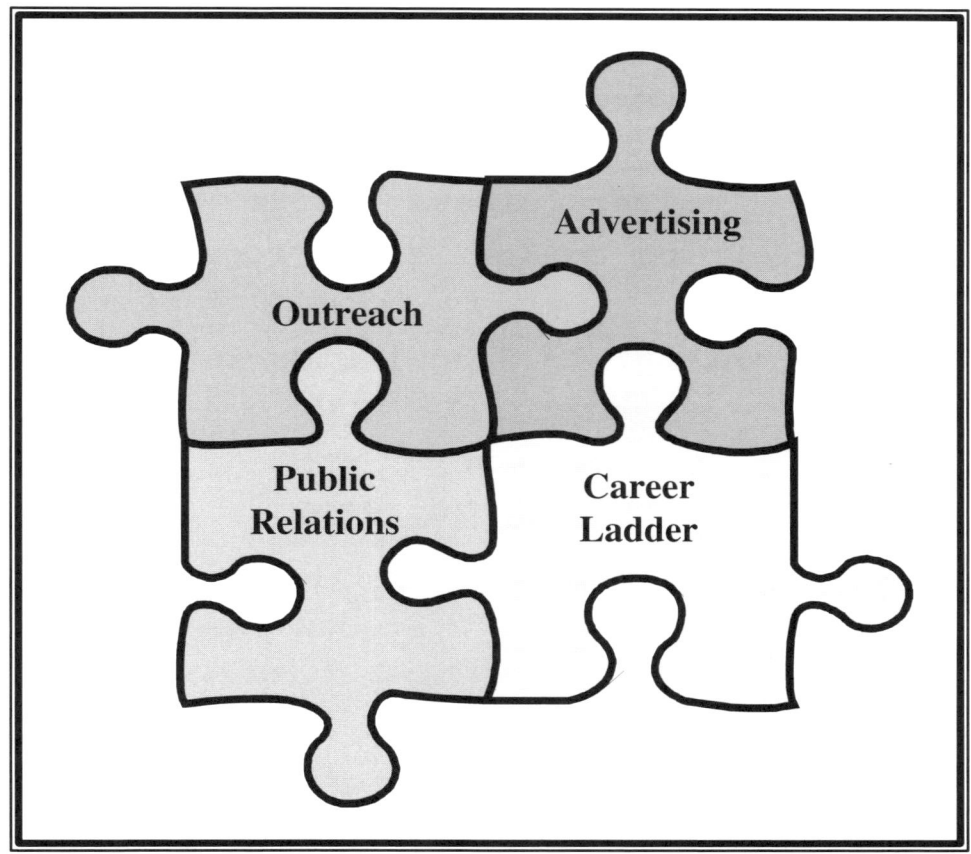

OUTREACH	Representatives of the district and task force participate in job fairs, recruitment fairs sponsored by colleges and universities, outplacement programs, outreach to community groups, and so forth.
ADVERTISING	Content, visual impact, and placement factors are always considered. Advertisements are placed in newspapers, educational journals, electronic media, placement agencies, radio, TV, and so forth.
PUBLIC RELATIONS	Brochures, district website, TV and radio interviews, newspaper coverage, guest lecturing at local colleges and universities regarding employment-seeking skills in education.
CAREER LADDER	Involves collaborating with local schools of higher education to recruit nontraditional candidates. Nontraditional candidates can include noncertificated staff, local parents, out-placed professionals from nonschool fields, Future Teachers of America and other service organizations, local community leaders, former homemakers, Labor Department resources.

Figure 2.5 Special Invitation

> **The Centerville School District**
> **Cordially Invites**
> **<Janice Smith>**
> **to Participate in Our**
> **"Getting to Know You" Program**
> **at**
> **Centerville School District**
> **Centerville, USA**
> **on**
> **February 20, 2002**
>
> Alternate Dates Are Available.
>
> Please RSVP by <February 10> to schedule arrangements.
>
> Stephanie Blair, Personnel Director
>
> 1-800-555-1111
>
> sblair@centerville.edu

interest candidates who met many of the district's criteria but who might not have explored a career with Centerville.

Outreach Highlight 2: The Getting to Know You Program

In the past, Centerville had focused so much on its own needs that it neglected to consider the work and family-community needs of new staff members who were unfamiliar with the local area. Therefore, Centerville sometimes failed to attract or retain the best qualified staff, especially candidates whose background was different from many people in Centerville.

"Getting to Know You" pairs candidates with a colleague from the prospective department or school. Through this program, the candidates visit classes, see the community, explore housing opportunities, attend events, and complete the interview process (see Figure 2.7). The role of the candidate is to explore how he or she might pursue a career and a life in Centerville. The role of the colleague is to get to know the candidate's needs, and to help the candidate meet those needs in the Centerville community.

The team had helped recruit and retain four staff members through this process: two secondary science teachers, an elementary teacher with reading certification, and a K-12 special educator. Two of these new staff members made their first contact with Centerville schools through the diversity recruitment fair and the other two were recruited at out-of-state college fairs. The personnel director highlighted four benefits of the "Getting to Know You" program:

1. Personal connections and friendships were made, which increase the rate of retention.
2. The candidates shared Centerville opportunities with other alumni of their schools, which expanded the network of potential candidates for positions in the district.
3. The district had more time to gauge the interpersonal skills and deep understandings presented by the candidate in a variety of settings.
4. The candidates were able to explore personal and family needs, such as child care, employment for a spouse, and so forth.

Advertisement Highlights

Advertisement is a key element of Building Block 2: Staffing. Advertising involves timing, content, and coordination with the other three staffing practices: outreach, public relations, and career ladder activities. The personnel director highlighted two advertising activities the task force used over the past three years. The first activity was a conventional print advertisement placed in the local and regional newspapers (Resource F). The second activity was an electronic posting that Centerville submitted to a regional organization of personnel directors who collaboratively posted "Emergency and Anticipated Openings" for all the schools who participated in this organization. Interested candidates would log onto the organization's website and follow the directions to apply for the posted positions.

The following are the basic criteria for advertisements that the task force created during the first year of their work:

1. Accurate and complete information proofread by at least two people
2. Efficient use of space
3. Ease of reading
4. Plain, standard language
5. Highly recognizable district logo always in the same location on the advertisement
6. Minimum requirements needed, including certifications and experience
7. Clear closing date
8. Specific instructions, including how the candidate should address and send the information and documents requested in the advertisement
9. Best possible placement in print, electronic, or other media.

Public Relations Highlights

After a careful cost-benefit analysis of previous public relations activities for recruiting new staff, the subcommittee on how to staff recommended that public relations–related resources should be carefully allocated in two directions:

1. Cultivate connections to preservice teacher education programs.
2. Extend the network of resources for new staff, including state and private university systems within and beyond the local area.

An example of reaching out to the local preservice network came from the director of the Languages Other Than English Department. He pointed out that new candidates were sending weak, confusing resumes and poorly constructed cover letters. Sometimes he could not tell what position the candidate was seeking, what credentials the candidate held, or even how to reach the candidate for an interview. The other members agreed.

The director collaborated with student teacher supervisors from several local colleges and universities. They offered a short resume and cover letter writing workshop for education department students attending local colleges and universities. Education department chairs welcomed the Centerville school's new service for prospective teachers. Resumes and cover letters submitted from students who completed the workshops consistently incorporated the top four criteria taught in the workshops:

1. State personal information first, including phone and email.
2. Indicate position sought second.
3. List relevant certifications and degrees third.
4. Give a brief chronology of relevant experience.

As a result of information from recent recruits, Centerville schools also decided to send a "What Can I Expect Next?" information packet to all candidates invited for interviews. The packet described key aspects of the Centerville induction process, from the initial interview to the hiring and orientation process, as well as some basic information about the mission and profile of the district.

Both of these public relations activities produced a measurable and growing impact on the quality and quantity of candidates.

Career Ladder Highlights

"Career ladder" refers to the first "rungs" a person who is not certified to teach can climb to achieve the status of a licensed, certificated educator. By way of example, the personnel director told the story of a person who started his career at Centerville as a custodian at the high school and is currently completing his first year as a technology teacher in the very same building. Through the collaborative efforts of the high school principal and other members of the district, the custodian completed his degree and certification requirements while continuing his employment on the custodial staff.

He was one of several former noncertificated staff members who had always aspired to teach, loved students, but had never had the opportunity to attend college and complete requirements necessary to become a teacher. He was just one of a growing number of staff members entering the profession through nontraditional routes. He joined the faculty at the same time as a teacher, who used the career ladder initiative to leave her position in business finance to become a math teacher at Centerville Middle School. This form of recruitment is a growing trend in schools and districts nationwide.

HOW TO INTERVIEW   ■

Note: Centerville has an initial screening committee, with subcommittees, that does much of the interviewing work. Candidates go through initial screening and meet people in their category (reading, secondary math, third grade). The size and complexity of districts vary too much to state all of the possibilities for interviews and demonstration lessons. Two things are crucial:

- Teachers must be involved in the interview process.
- The principal or immediate supervisor must be involved in the process.

The elementary principal, chair of the How to Interview Subcommittee, presented four highlights:

1. Connecting Interviewing to Recruiting: The Applicant Pool
2. Team building
3. Interviewing According to Nine Standards of Professional Practice
4. Recommending Finalist Status and Hiring the Candidate

As the elementary principal described each of these highlights, she related each one to Centerville's nine standards of professional practice (see Figure 2.6).

Highlight 1: Connecting Interviewing to Recruiting: The Applicant Pool

"We received the best applicant pool in years," the principal said. "For example, we received approximately 15 percent more resumes from qualified candidates in the first year of our initiative than we did before we instituted our new approach to induction. We had the greatest increases in our 'hard to staff areas' such as science, math, technology, and languages other than English. We defined 'qualified' as having the correct degrees and certifications. That made the interviewing process much more efficient and productive, all around."

Highlight 2: Team Building

"In this highlight, we are referring to the facilitator's team-building activities for all committees involved in either setting the standards for interviewing or actually conducting building-based interviews," the elementary principal said. "The facilitator helped everyone understand three basic things:

- The role of the How to Interview Subcommittee: to set the standards for the building-based interview committees
- The role of each building-based interview committee: to screen and ultimately recommend candidates
- The strategies any committee members could use to raise issues, debate perspectives, and reach consensus"

Figure 2.6 Nine Standards of Professional Practice

The Core of Our Recruitment, Supervision, Observation, Evaluation, and Recognition Program
The educator demonstrates proficiency in:

1. Content area(s) and standards
2. Instructional delivery
3. Classroom management and discipline
4. Knowledge of student characteristics and needs
5. Planning and preparation
6. Collaboration
7. Reflective and responsive practices
8. Evaluation/assessment of student learning
9. Professional conduct and demeanor

Highlight 3: Interviewing According to Nine Standards of Professional Practice

The nine standards (Figure 2.6) were familiar to all the members of the audience because they were the same criteria used to observe and evaluate all the professional staff at Centerville School District.

The elementary school principal cautioned the audience to remember, "By using the nine standards during all phases of the interview process, we helped ensure that the candidates we recommended as finalists for hiring demonstrated the standards we set for our entire professional staff. We understood that entry-level staff would not necessarily demonstrate mastery of all the areas of professional practice, but we did expect candidates to demonstrate evidence or potential in each of the nine areas. Of course, we also wanted them to know the district's nine standards." (Note: This is very important for any district. You might have five or seven or ten standards for excellence, but they should be formulated by a broad-based group and made known to candidates.)

After the elementary school principal led the task force through key elements of Figure 2.7, Tips for Completing a Successful Interview Process, she pointed out that these new questions generated more substantive responses than interview committees were accustomed to receiving in the past. The responses, in turn, generated lively, productive discussions during the candidate review.

"Watch this clip of just one discussion that one interview committee allowed us to film. Look for how the group used the facilitator's suggested strategies to:

- Raise issues;
- Identify the candidate's strengths and weaknesses according to the standards set by the How to Interview Subcommittee;
- Achieve consensus regarding how closely this candidate would match the district's needs and goals. The consensus process really kept us focused on making the right decisions for the right reasons."

Figure 2.7   Tips for Completing a Successful Interview Process

I.	Tips for Screening Resumes and Cover Letters

(a)   Look for:
- Degrees, licenses/certifications
- Relevant experience
- Academic institutions and degree programs
- Qualifications to coach/lead extracurricular or cocurricular activities
- Computer literacy
- Presentation of resume and cover letter
- Examples: spelling, punctuation, and grammar
- Other leadership/community service roles
- Fluency in languages other than English
- Strengths or characteristics in other areas that match district initiatives

(b)   Look out for:
- Gaps in employment history
- Frequent changes in employment

II.	Tips for Inviting Applicants to Interviews

(a)   Make sure that interview times are available day and evening
(b)   Use respectful, professional, welcoming practices throughout the entire interview process, from the initial contact to the final recommendation.

III.	Tips for Designing and Evaluating Oral and Written Questions

(a)   Could be targeted to specific areas, such as an applicant for:
- High school guidance to compose a letter of recommendation for a student
- Elementary reading to write a letter to a parent explaining a child's progress and describing the reading services the school will provide to the child
- Middle school science teacher to describe how writing and reading skills are part of the science program

(b)   Provide each applicant with the opportunity to respond to more than one question for the writing sample.
(c)   Ask only those questions that conform to federal, state, and local guidelines (federal restrictions include asking questions about such topics as marital status, age, income, children/family issues, disabilities, ethnicity, sexual orientation, religion, and so forth).

IV.	Sample Questions for Oral or Written Interview

(a)   Ask questions that reflect Centerville's purpose: To Help All Students Learn Well and Stay Safe
- "How would you differentiate instruction for the variety of learners you might have in your classroom? Please give us examples."

(Continued)

Figure 2.7 *(Continued)*

- "Imagine that it is the change of classes in middle school. Your supervisor has asked you to remain visible in the hall by your classroom as students pass from one period to another. How would you make contact with your own students as they entered your class and still comply with your principal's request?"
- "Help us understand how you would choose or create your personal professional development plan?"
- "Please share with us how you would integrate technology into a lesson. Give a specific example using a content area and actual lesson you might teach."
- "How would you collaborate with a parent to help a student follow school or classroom procedures? What would you do first, next, and so forth?

After the clip was over, the elementary school principal asked a task force member, also on that particular interview committee, to share their "change of heart" interviewing experiences. A teacher explained that he was sure that a substitute he had enjoyed working with would interview well. In fact, the candidate interviewed less confidently than another candidate unknown to the district. At first, he was inclined to remove the substitute's name from advancement in the process. He was surprised when more veteran members of the committee reminded him that the first rule of the interview process is to keep the interview in perspective. It is just one element of the entire picture of a candidate.

"At that point, I changed my mind and agreed with the rest of the committee—that the candidate's writing sample, experience, and interview—together—really should advance her to the next level. I learned two very important things here—that interviewing is an imperfect part of a larger process, and that I should not expect more of a person I worked with than I might expect of any other candidate in any interview."

As it happened, the committee was able to videotape a demonstration lesson, since Candidate 23 signed a release permitting the district to use it for in-district staff development purposes only. The video was taped so that only the backs of the students were visible to the observer to protect the identity of the children in the class.

After the task force members viewed the video clip, the elementary school principal led the committee through a quick activity comparing their own observations of the "demo" lesson with the notes on the grid (Figure 2.8, Guidelines for Preparing the Candidate for a Demonstration

Figure 2.8   Guidelines for Preparing the Candidate for a Demonstration
Lesson

What?	Who?	Why?
Seating chart provided to candidate	Demonstration Lesson Evaluators	To help the candidate engage learners
Evaluator's Rating Scale (See Figure 2.10)		To help the candidate understand the criteria for assessment
Appropriate text, materials, etc.		To help the candidate refer students to prior and future learning
Previous day's lesson		To build on prior learning
Exact timeframe for demo lesson (30 minutes; 20 minutes, etc.?)		To pace the lesson appropriately
Expected content, including learning standards for students		To ensure that the demo lesson reflects district curriculum.
The nine professional standards of practice Centerville uses to supervise, observe and evaluate teachers		To help the candidate use the professional practices most valued and measured by the district 1. Content area(s) 2. Instructional delivery 3. Classroom management 4. Knowledge of student characteristics and needs 5. Preparation 6. Collaboration 7. Reflective and responsive practices 8. Evaluation/assessment of student learning 9. Professional conduct and demeanor
Special Circumstances: Example: Fire Drill scheduled; special bell schedules, students with disabilities/ special needs		To help the candidate and the students do their best. To meet basic learning and safety goals.

Figure 2.9 Guidelines for Evaluating a Candidate's Demonstration Lesson

Rated on a scale of 1–5:
_____1. Little/no evidence
_____2. Some evidence
_____3. Shows evidence
_____4. Shows strong evidence
_____5. Not applicable

RATING	COMMENTS (Using Language of the Nine Standards)	CRITERIA
		Stated learner objective
		Indicated learning standard and key idea. (Student) Example: math/measurement
		Provided appropriate input (new learning)
		Provided guided and/or independent/interdependent practice
		Monitored, assessed, and provided appropriate feedback to students regarding learning and conduct
		Completed closure
		Indicated appropriate homework
		Used appropriate materials
		Engaged students in appropriate activities
		Used appropriately varied teaching strategies, including questioning techniques and skills
		Used appropriately varied management strategies
		Established a safe, welcoming, orderly environment where students would freely participate
		Students were academically engaged

Lesson) used by the actual interview committee. As the committee compared observations, the school social worker was the first to observe that the task force members and interview committee reports matched on most of the highlighted items. "If you look down the list," the school social worker pointed out, "you can see right away that we all agreed that Candidate 23 was highly skilled in the areas of content, delivery of instruction, classroom management, and knowledge of student characteristics/needs."

The elementary principal reported that the interview committee had advanced Candidate 23 to the next level. She illustrated how the committee decided to advance the candidate by referring to the candidate's Review for Selection Packet (see Figure 2.11). The packet contained the candidate's:

- Cover letter
- Certification(s)
- Resume
- Writing sample
- Interview results
- Evaluations of the demonstration lesson

The committee members used all of the material listed above to make their recommendation for advancing Candidate 23 to the third and final phase of interviewing: checking professional references. The Review for Selection Packet continues to "follow" the candidate from the beginning to the end of his or her recruitment, interviewing and hiring process.

At this point, the elementary school principal spoke about the procedure they adopted to make reference checks before recommending any candidate for "finalist" status. "We learn so much about our candidates from checking references," she began. "We learned that we have to listen very carefully to two different messages when a reference communicates with us over the phone or in print. We have to listen and read for what the referring source says and does not say about the candidate. If the reference does not respond at all, that might be a message in itself. Be careful. Use the phone to check."

"Several candidates did go through the interview and demonstration process, only to be eliminated after checking references. We used the 'Confidential Telephone Reference Check' (Figure 2.10) so everyone followed the same procedures and asked the same questions. If you scan it quickly, you'll notice Item 8: 'Is there any question I should have asked but didn't, or is there anyone else I should speak with about this candidate?'"

"Continuing to follow the success story of Candidate 23, we decided to advance the candidate to finalist status. As a result, the principal of the building where the candidate would be working collected all the materials required for the Review for Selection Packet." Most committees have the principal collect materials. This process ensures that:

- The packet is in the hands of one person.
- The principal sees the entire folder.
- The job is done by a person with office equipment and a secretary.

The elementary school principal showed the list in Figure 2.11 to help the committee members see what items to include in the Review for Selection Packet.

Figure 2.10 Confidential Telephone Reference Check

Confidential

CENTERVILLE SCHOOL DISTRICT

Certificated Telephone Reference Check

Candidate_____ Considered Position_____

Person Providing Reference_____ Title_____

Organization_____Phone (   )_____

Guidelines

1. Screening check must be done on the final candidate prior to recommendation to Personnel.

2. A minimum of two telephone or personal reference checks must be made. At least one should be at the supervisory level, preferably the most immediate past supervisor.

3. All comments must be legible and complete.

4. All reference checks must be performed uniformly.

5. Note to caller: If the person declines to answer the reference check questions, ask if he/she would please respond to the following brief statement:

It is the policy of this district to only verify basic information such as length of employment, job title, etc. _____Yes _____No

Period employed from _____to_____

Job Title _____

1. How long and in what capacity have you known this applicant? Look for: Knows candidate in a professional or work capacity for at least six months.

    _____
    _____

2. How would you rate the applicant's knowledge and application of appropriate instructional techniques? What is the basis for this rating?

    _____
    _____
    _____

3. How would you rate the applicant's ability to work as a member of an educational team? What is the basis of your rating?

    _____

    _____

4. Please identify this candidate's greatest asset as an employee.
    Look for: Assets that match specific skills needed for the position. Strong interpersonal skills, dependable, flexible, quality worker, team player.

    _____

    _____

    _____

5. Please identify any concerns.

    Look for: No Concerns.

    _____

    _____

6. If this person no longer works for you, what was the reason for leaving, and would you hire him/her again?

    Look for: Positive reason for leaving. Positive response to rehire; no hesitation.

    _____

    _____

7. Do you know of any reason why the applicant should not be employed to work around students?

    Look for: No reasons.

    _____

    _____

8. Is there anything I should have asked, but didn't, anyone else I should speak with or additional information you would like to share with me?

    Look for: No negative comments.

    _____

    _____

References checked by_____Date_____

    This information is being gathered solely for the purpose of determining appropriate hiring for the specific position. All responses shall be regarded as confidential and shall not be used for any other purpose.

Figure 2.11   Items for "Review for Selection Packet" in Order of the Candidate's Progress

---

Level One: Items Included During Recruiting Phase

_____ A.   Candidate's cover letter

_____ B.   Resume

_____ C.   Transcripts

_____ D.   Copies of certifications or material in lieu of certification

Level Two: Items Included During Interviewing Phase

_____ E.   Completed writing samples

_____ F.   Evaluation sheets from the building-based interview committee members

_____ G.   Evaluation sheets from those who observed the demonstration lesson

Level Three: Items to Be Included During the Hiring Phase

_____ H.   Telephone check of professional references

_____ I.   Memo written by the building principal recommending the candidate(s) to be moved forward to central office interview

_____ J.   Candidate's district application form

_____ K.   Letter of intent/binder signed by candidate with recommended salary

_____ L.   Memo to board of education from superintendent recommending that the candidate be hired

---

Highlight 4: Recommanding Finalist Status and Hiring the Candidate

The high school principal opened this fourth and last section of the task force meeting by making the connections among the three elements of staffing:

- Recruiting
- Interviewing
- Hiring

"In this last portion of our meeting, we'll share how we staff by hiring the best candidates that we have recruited and interviewed. We all just observed Candidate 23's interview, complete with demonstration lesson and reference check. Now we're going to illustrate the hiring phase a little differently. If you look at your How to Hire Flow Chart (Figure 2.12), you can see that we follow a sequence of steps to hire a member of our Centerville instructional staff."

"As you look at Step B and Step C detailing the steps of the Central Office Review, notice that they both refer to 'two candidates' for each position referred at this level." At this point, the high school principal reminded the task force that the school district's policy is to recommend two equally qualified candidates for every position. He clarified that this policy has three benefits.

Figure 2.12   "How to Hire" Flowchart

	"HOW TO HIRE" STEP A The interview committee and building principal recommend the candidates who will meet with one or more central office-level administrators to complete the "Review for Selection."	
	"HOW TO HIRE" STEP B Personnel office receives the packets (see Figure 2.11) and reviews credentials/references of the final two candidates being recommended for the "Review for Selection."	

	"HOW TO HIRE" STEP C
	Two candidates for each position are advanced to Central Office-Level "Review for Selection." This review may be conducted by one or more of the individuals listed below:
	- Superintendent
	- Assistant Superintendent or Director of:
	  • Curriculum and Instruction
	  • Personnel
	  • Special Education
	  • Pupil Personnel Services
	  • Elementary Education or Secondary Education	

	"HOW TO HIRE" STEP D After the final candidate is chosen, the Personnel Director or other central office administrator will review the following items with the candidate: - Salary - Payroll procedures - Benefits - Date and procedures for appointment in public session of the Board of Education - Orientation goals and schedule - Particulars of the Letter of Intent/Binder (Resource D) - Procedures for completing district forms	
	"HOW TO HIRE" STEP E Personnel Director (PD) sends "Review for Selection" packet to Superintendent. Memo from PD to Superintendent recommending candidate for appointment includes: - Recommendation for job title/position - Salary and "step/level" - Probationary status - Building - Starting date and ending date Additional material in the packet includes: application, writing sample, transcript, copy of certification(s): - Binding letter of intent signed by the candidate binds the candidate to the district, not the district to the candidate - Recommendations from the Interview Committee - Recommendations from PD - Credentials and references - Other relevant materials	
	"HOW TO HIRE" STEP F: APPROVAL - Superintendent sends his or her recommendations to the Board of Education. - Board of Education votes on the recommendations in an Open Meeting. The candidate is invited to attend the board meeting, and spouses/children may be invited to attend. - The Personnel Director may acknowledge all the candidates at once, or each in turn. - The day after the Board of Education confirms the appointment, the Personnel Director sends out a letter of appointment (Resource E).	

First, the hiring process is more equitable. This procedure advances equity by protecting against some of the favoritism we all know can surface during hiring. Second, it brings the central office into the process. Third, it is more efficient. If a final candidate declines an offer or another position suddenly opens in the same area in our own district, the district has another qualified candidate to fill the position immediately.

The assistant superintendent quickly acknowledged that having two strong candidates for each position can make it difficult to choose. "The final reference check that you see in Hiring Step B is sometimes the deciding factor. Each year, we are all astounded at how many things we learn about our candidates right up to the last minutes of our decision-making process."

"The Review for Selection that you see in Hiring Step C is a unique opportunity for central office administrators to discover more about the candidate than the traditional interview can generally reveal. This is an opportunity for the candidate to share his or her professional dreams and goals—for the candidate and the district to get to know one another, so to speak."

Typically, the central office administrator might try to learn more about the person by asking such questions as the following, because these kinds of questions can be the basis of a dialogue.

What traits or characteristics make you stand out above the members of your graduating class?

What was your most rewarding student-teaching experience?

Share how you have been affected by a teacher when you were in school.

Who is a hero to you? Why?

What do you think the role of a teacher is in the life of a child?

What questions do you have about teaching here in Centerville schools?

What are some things you plan to do to become part of our Centerville "team"?

"There are no right or wrong answers to questions posed at the Review for Selection level. We're trying to get to know the candidate, to see how she or he expresses thoughts and feelings in response to our questions. We're asking these questions to share what we value, and to discover what the candidate values."

"Hiring," the high school principal concluded, "is my favorite part of the whole recruitment process. It's the moment when you finally get to tell a candidate, 'Join us! You're our choice! And thanks for choosing us! This isn't just the beginning of your career; it is the beginning of a lifetime of connections with Centerville.'"

■ CHAPTER SUMMARY

This chapter was designed to help you achieve staffing goals. The chapter first illustrated how to use team-building strategies to prepare for staffing. Next, the chapter provided a sequence of steps to implement the recruitment, interviewing, and hiring elements of your staffing process, so you can attract and retain the best qualified staff for your school or district.

Tips

Connections

- Post dates for districtwide or building meetings in readily accessible locations and publications, including your district website, newsletter, and bulletin boards.
- Distribute agendas for districtwide and building meetings in advance of the meeting date.
- Organize meetings in ways that account for participants' comfort needs, including such factors as location, temperature, food, beverages, and restroom requirements.
- (And **Personnel Issues**) Share your staffing needs with all staff members, so they can always be active, informal recruiters for your school or district.

Data Mining

- (And **Personnel Issues**) Maintain a central repository of excellent student observers, student teachers or substitute teachers.

Finance

- Publicize as many openings as possible at the same time. It is more efficient and cost-effective to place advertisements and use public relations resources.
- Use an open-bidding process to discover the most cost-effective sources for placing advertisements.

Legal Issues

- (And **Personnel Issues**) Include at least two members of your district or school in each interview setting. This procedure protects the process for all concerned.
- (And **Professional Development**) Ensure that all members of your interview committees are informed about how to phrase and ask questions within the confines of what is legal. You may achieve this goal by involving your interviewers in informational meetings and role-playing activities with your district's attorney, so they can practice phrasing questions appropriately.
- (And **Personnel Issues**) Circulate the How to Hire/Steps to Hiring Flow Chart (Figure 2.12) to all those who participate in the hiring process. By following this tip, all participants in the hiring process know what steps have preceded their role, and where the candidate must go once they have finished.

Personnel Issues

- Ask candidates about why they want to work in your district in particular. This can help you discover those candidates who have researched and learned about your district or school.

- Keep candidate-related information material in one packet and in one area.

Professional Development

- Engage your interview teams in professional development activities to help them use the same schoolwide or districtwide standards of practice.
- Include professional staff from each school building in your district, so you have a wide variety of educators prepared to participate in staffing activities.

■ NOTES

1. Carver, J. (1997). *Boards that make a difference*. San Francisco: Jossey-Bass.

2. Csikszentmihalyi, M. (1997). *Finding flow: The psychology of engagement with everyday life*. New York: Basic Books.

3. Please see Resource B: Leading for Learning and Safety: A Leadership Development Institute.

BLUEPRINT FOR BUILDING BLOCK 2

Building Block 2	GOALS	PARTICIPANTS	OBJECTIVES	NEXT STEPS
	STAFFING: Recruiting Interviewing Hiring			
__2a	Staffing Committee convenes to: • Use BluePrint to make decisions • Identify objectives	Members should include representatives from: • Administration • Other educators • Parent/community	Establish subcommittees on: • Recruiting • Interviewing Assess need for training/development regarding staffing	Conduct training/development as needed Each subcommittee arranges: • Meeting dates • Activities consistent with the BluePrint
	Recruiting			
__2b	Recruiting subcommittee convenes	Personnel director and others as appropriate	Gather and organize data regarding staffing needs over coming year(s)	• Use the staffing projections to prepare a recruitment plan that helps the district achieve its learning and safety goals • Monitor/assess/report progress
__2c	Outreach subcommittee meets	• Personnel director • Members of the Recruitment Subcommittee	To reach out to nontraditional and traditional resources for educators consistent with staffing needs/goals	Coordinate outreach with advertising, public relations, and career ladder activities

(Continued)

	GOALS	PARTICIPANTS	OBJECTIVES	NEXT STEPS
__2d	Advertising subcommittee meets to set objectives	• Personnel director • Members of the Recruitment Subcommittee	To attract the best candidates to meet staffing needs/goals	Coordinate with outreach, public relations and career ladder activities
__2e	Public Relations subcommittee meets to set objectives	• Personnel director • Members of the Recruitment Subcommittee	To attract the best candidates to meet staffing needs/goals	Coordinate with outreach, public relations and career ladder activities
__2f	Career Ladder subcommittee meets to set objectives	• Personnel director • Members of the Recruitment Subcommittee	To attract the best candidates to meet staffing needs/goals	Coordinate with outreach, public relations, and career ladder activities
__2g	Sustain the interviewing, hiring, and appointing process until all staffing needs are met.	• Personnel director • Other district and building/department/grade-level leaders • Interview teams	To recommend at least two equally qualified professional candidates for each available position	Use the data to make recommendations regarding the staffing initiative for the following year(s)
Interviewing				
__2h	Interviewing subcommittee convenes to set objectives	Members	To complete training in I:CRR approach to interviewing	Plan the sequence of activities for: • Reviewing resumes • Interviewing • Evaluating demonstration lessons • Achieving consensus regarding making recommendations to move candidates forward toward hiring

	GOALS	PARTICIPANTS	OBJECTIVES	NEXT STEPS
__ 2i	Reviewing resumes	Members	Find best candidates for each position	Use data from resumes to select and schedule candidates
__ 2j	Using interview questioning techniques	Members	Evaluate candidates fairly on the same criteria	Use data from interview to select candidates for the demonstration lessons
__ 2k	Evaluating demonstration lessons	Members	Use standards of professional practice and criteria from the district's observation and evaluation program to evaluate demonstration lessons	• Use data from the demonstration lesson, interview, resume, etc., to advance selected candidates to the hiring phase • Prepare candidate's Review for Selection Packet
__ 2l	Interviewers send finalists to building, departmental, and/or central office interview stage	Could include: • Central office staff • Personnel director • Building principal • Department chair	Interviewers achieve consensus regarding recommendations to move candidates forward to the personnel director and superintendent	Superintendent follows district policy and board goals
	Hiring			
__ 2m	Superintendent recommends the most qualified candidates to the board of education	• Board of education • Superintendent • Personnel director	The board of education appoints the candidates that the superintendent recommends	Superintendent, personnel director, and others lead the district to take next steps toward retaining the newly recruited educators

See Appendix A for the Complete BluePrint for all five Building Blocks to Induction

3

Orienting New Members of Your Professional Staff

Year One

THIS CHAPTER WILL HELP YOU

- Implement a year-long orientation program
- Create connections for first-year staff
- Help first-year staff learn school and district policies, practices, and procedures
- Align the orientation program with your:
  - Professional development activities
  - Supervision, observation, and evaluation program

As Superintendent Frasier acknowledged the dedication of his veteran staff and recognized his newly tenured staff, Dan Hammond stood to be recognized as a tenured member of the

Centerville professional staff. He recalled how nervous he was just three years ago, when he first stood to be recognized as a newly hired member of the district. Back then, he felt overwhelmed. Today, as he looked around the auditorium, he saw many colleagues who had become friends over these past three years. Taking his seat, he felt confident that he had made the right decision when he accepted the position with Centerville School District.

When the assembly program ended, Dan joined a few colleagues to pick up their Professional Portfolios (Figure 3.1) from the personnel office. They were among twelve newly tenured educators the task force asked to offer their thoughts and suggestions regarding at least one Building Block from Centerville's induction initiative. They were encouraged to

- Select materials from their portfolios that highlight their experiences during the orienting or connecting stages of their induction
- Make specific suggestions to refine and improve the induction process
- Present those suggestions to the Induction Task Force

All Centerville Professional Portfolios were organized to correspond to the five Building Blocks for Induction. Within that framework, each portfolio was unique since each included materials the educator selected to represent his or her best professional practices at each stage of induction. Centerville required all probationary teachers to maintain a Professional Portfolio.

Dan decided to highlight his experiences during Building Block 3: Orienting. This chapter features those highlights.

Dan decided to begin his assessment of his first year of induction with the chart all new teachers received when they were hired (see Figure 3.2), outlining the benchmarks of induction from appointment to tenure. The chart gave a "snapshot" view of what Centerville School District would do to support him through an integrated program of formal observation, evaluation, and professional development.

PREORIENTATION: CONNECTING BEFORE THE SCHOOL YEAR APPOINTMENT BEGINS

In the months between Dan's appointment and the date he started teaching, Centerville School District offered him several opportunities to participate as an active member of the school community. They encouraged him to attend professional activities and introduced him to local real estate contacts.

In assessing the school district's approach to the preorientation part of Building Block 3, he decided to highlight three significant best practices

(text continues on p. 50)

Figure 3.1 Creating and Maintaining a Professional Portfolio

What is a Professional Portfolio?	A portfolio: 1. Is the product of self-reflection in the context of the school's mission and professional standards of practice; 2. Includes key elements and examples of a plan the educator and supervisor(s) develop and refine to help the educator set and achieve goals identified through the supervision, observation, and evaluation process; 3. Is a place where an educator can document the link between professional practice and student performance.
Why maintain a Professional Portfolio?	A professional portfolio is valuable to maintain because it: 1. Fosters and focuses practices associated with being a reflective and responsive educator 2. Helps the educator use the same criteria and standards as administrators to assess the educator's professional practices 3. Reflects changes and developments during the educator's career 4. Helps new and veteran educators make clear connections between self-assessment and evidence of student learning and safety
Who should maintain a Professional Portfolio?	1. Every probationary teacher 2. All post-tenure/permanence educators in five-year cycles
Who will review the Professional Portfolio?	1. For tenure? The educator who creates it, the educator's mentor, and the supervisor (the building principal, central office administrator) 2. Once an educator has earned tenure/permanence? The educator and at least one supervisor
When will the Professional Portfolio be reviewed?	1. For tenure? Every year during probationary period 2. Once an educator has earned tenure/permanence? Every five years
Why review a Professional Portfolio?	All good practice is measured according to standards set by the district.
How should a Professional Portfolio be organized?	The Professional Portfolio should be organized into five major sections corresponding to Building Blocks 1 through 5.

(Continued)

Figure 3.1 *(Continued)*

What should be included in a portfolio?	**BUILDING BLOCK 1—*Preparing***
	Centerville School District
	Mission Statement
	Induction Policy
	Benchmarks for Probationary Educators:
	From Appointment to Tenure (Figure 3.2)

BUILDING BLOCK 1—*Preparing*

Centerville School District
    Mission Statement
    Induction Policy
    Benchmarks for Probationary Educators:
      From Appointment to Tenure (Figure 3.2)

- Self-Reflective Statement A: "How I Intend to Help Advance the Mission"
- Self-Reflective Statement B: "How I Have Helped to Advance Centerville School District's Mission to Help All Students Learn Well and Stay Safe"

BUILDING BLOCK 2—*Staffing*

    Educator-selected elements of personal "Review for Selection Packet"

- Examples: Resume, Transcripts, Recommendations, Copies of Certifications/Degrees, Letter of Appointment

BUILDING BLOCK 3—*Orienting*

    Educator-selected elements of participation in each of the following:

- Preorientation Activities: Only Preceding Year 1
  - Examples could include participation in any related activity
- Professional Development Year 1:
  - Examples could include highlights of orientation, monthly meetings, coursework, and so forth within and beyond Core Curriculum (Figure 3.6)
- Mentoring/Collaboration Year 1:
  - Examples could include highlights of mentor/mentee activities, including lessons, co-planning materials, and so forth
- Supervision, Observation, and Evaluation Year 1
  - Formal: Examples could include sample lessons/units, student performance results, and observations/evaluations that show growth
  - Informal: Examples could include letters, notes, memos, student work, parent communications, and so forth

BUILDING BLOCK 4—*Connecting*

    Educator-selected elements of participation in each of the following:

What should be included in a portfolio?	• Continuing professional development, Years 2-3:
	  • Coursework and other activities within and beyond the core curriculum
	• Continuing mentoring/collaborating, Years 2-3
	  • Fulfilling the role of the mentee
	• Continuing supervision, observation, and evaluation, Years 2-3
	  • Formal: Examples could include sample lessons and units, student performance results, and observations/evaluations that show growth
	  • Informal: Examples could include letters from parents or students, notes, memos, student work, parent communications, log of experiences, samples of student work, interdisciplinary instructional activities, thematic units, and so forth
	• Granting tenure/permanence
	  • Building Principal's letter to the superintendent recommending tenure/permanence
	  • Building principal's tenure/permanence evaluation, indicating that the educator has met or exceeded the nine standards of professional practice (Figure 2.6)
	  • Superintendent's letter to the board of education recommending tenure/permanence
	
	BUILDING BLOCK 5—*Retaining/Reorienting*
	Educator-selected elements of participation in each of the following:
	• Sustaining the connection
	  • Examples can include materials from mentoring, workshops taught and attended, collaborations, conferences, and so forth
	• Supervising, observing, and evaluating career-long learning:
	  • Examples can include observations, evaluations, formal and informal comments from peers, supervisors, model lessons, and so forth
	• Renewing and reorienting:
	  • Examples can include materials from Reorientation Program activities

Figure 3.2 Benchmarks From Appointment to Tenure

	Year One: BB3: Orienting	Year Two: BB4: Connecting	Year Three: BB4: Connecting
Preorientation	X		
Summer orientation	X		
Monthly workshops	X		
End of school year workshops	X	X	X
Observations (minimum: four formal observations per year)	X	X	X
Mid-year evaluations	X	X	X
End of year evaluations	X	X	X
Tenure/permanence appointment			X

the district used to help new educators become members of the school community:[1]

- Housing help
- District orientation packet and invitations to attend district functions
- Building orientation packet and invitations to attend building and departmental functions

Preorientation Best Practice: Housing Help

Dan reviewed the memo the personnel director had written offering special tips to meet his family's housing needs. He did first rent and then purchase a home in a nearby community that was one of the places recommended. He recalled that this help made it possible for him to focus on the professional practices that Centerville emphasized.

Preorientation Best Practice: District Orientation Packet

Dan first began to understand Centerville's strong emphasis on professional practices when he received the Centerville District Orientation Packet, which included:

- The dates and agenda for the Summer Orientation Program, which was required of all educators new to Centerville
- A Professional Portfolio binder divided into five sections corresponding to the Building Blocks of Induction
- An outline of the core curriculum for all Centerville educators

- A copy of the Professional Development/Course Offerings Handbook for the summer and fall sessions, listing all courses, dates, times, locations, prerequisites, and facilitators
- An updated list of district and community events a new educator might want to attend
- A district calendar

From the moment he opened that orientation packet, he felt he was a member of the school community. The materials were organized and comprehensive, so he knew exactly what the district expected of him, and what he could expect of the district. The newly tenured teacher used those resources to:

- Make the right professional decisions for the right reasons
- Help him apply Centerville's standards of professional practice (see Figure 2.6) when selecting examples to include in his Professional Portfolio
- Become an increasingly reflective and responsive educator

Preorientation Best Practice: Building Orientation Packet

Just after Dan received the District Orientation Packet, he received a mailing from his high school principal. This mailing was a Building Orientation Packet that included schedules for department meetings, faculty meetings, building events, and a building calendar for the new school year.

In the cover letter, the high school principal welcomed him to the building and invited him to attend a series of activities that would be taking place toward the end of the school year. Dan was invited as a new member of the school community but was not required to attend. The list of activities ranged from faculty meetings to awards assemblies and graduation. Dan chose to attend the following:

- The Transitional Orientation Program for parents and incoming 9th grade students, conducted by the Guidance Department
- A department review of student performance on assessments, facilitated by the department chair
- A special summer orientation "event" jointly conducted by the Centerville High School assistant principal and the building representative of the Centerville Teachers Association

Dan used these examples to illustrate how quickly and effectively Centerville helped him become an involved participant in the school community before he spent one day as a teacher.

Then he turned his attention to highlights of professional development activities he completed during Building Block 3: Orienting. He decided to focus on professional development activities in the actual order of their occurrence.

■ CONDUCTING PROFESSIONAL DEVELOPMENT

Once preorientation activities ended, the first year of professional development progressed in three major phases (see Figure 3.2):

- Summer orientation for educators entering their first year at Centerville
- Districtwide monthly meetings for educators in their first year at Centerville
- End-of-the-school-year workshops and seminars for all probationary educators

Dan decided to review the materials from each of these three phases in order of their occurrence and to show how the district, building, and departmental professional development activities were all aligned with each other.

Conducting Professional Development Best Practice: Summer Orientation Program

Dan selected the entire summer orientation program as a best practice since it helped him:

- Feel welcome and respected as a new member of a strong professional community
- Meet administrators and teachers from around the district
- Learn that Centerville School District expected all educators to follow specific standards of professional practice (see Figure 2.6)
- Explore how he could advance the Centerville mission in his daily practices
- Discover that all Centerville professional development was based on the same core curriculum of professional practices
- Affirm what was expected of him

Dan then included the agenda (Figure 3.3) for the summer orientation program in the materials he would use for his report to the Task Force on Induction. He listed the strengths of the summer orientation program and made one suggestion that he felt could improve the program overall. He believed that the district should allocate more time to lesson planning and instructional delivery, since those skills are so fundamental to a new educator's success.

Conducting Professional Development Best Practice: Monthly Meetings

Dan recalled how overwhelmed he was when he discovered that all educators new to the district had to attend districtwide monthly meetings during the first year of probation. He remembered thinking that he would never have enough time to do everything and be everywhere. He had

Figure 3.3 Agenda for the Summer Orientation Program for Educators New to Centerville

TIME	MONDAY	TUESDAY	WEDNESDAY	THURSDAY	FRIDAY
8:00 a.m.– 8:30 a.m.	Breakfast	Breakfast	Breakfast	Breakfast	Breakfast
8:30 a.m.– 11:30 a.m.	1. Welcome to Centerville by superintendent, teacher, and community member 2. Overview of the agenda for the week 3. Using Your Professional Portfolio to reflect on and respond to best practices 4. Centerville School District framework (Figure 1.2)	Focus on: Lesson Planning	Focus on: Assessment	Focus on: Student Conduct School Safety Connecting Character to Conduct Discipline Issues	Focus on: Professional Conduct–The Ninth Domain of Professional Practice
11:30 a.m.– 2.30 p.m.	Lunch	Lunch	Lunch	Lunch	Lunch

(Continued)

Figure 3.3 *(Continued)*

12:30 p.m.–3:30 p.m.	Focus on: Instructional Delivery and Classroom Management		Focus on: Using District Forms Home–School Communications
1. Walk through core curriculum and nine standards of professional practice (Figure 2.6) 2. How our S/O/E practices match our core curriculum and our framework 3. Using best practices to help all students learn well and stay safe, including students with disabilities or gifts		Bus tour of the district, OSHA and sexual harassment seminars	Next steps: "Introduction to Mentoring" Teacher association greeting and so forth

rarely found end-of-the-day meetings or classes very productive, and he was not optimistic about this requirement.

He was relieved to discover that the meetings were mostly interactive, with many practical, hands-on activities. The topics were timely, the facilitators were knowledgeable, and they were usually experienced Centerville administrators or veteran teachers. The monthly meetings helped him refine and use professional practices that promoted learning and safety.

During his first year of teaching, the following topics were presented at the monthly meetings:

Month 1: Back to School/Meet the Teacher/Home-School Communications

Month 2: Grading and Interim Reports

Month 3: Working Together with Parents and Colleagues

Month 4: Our Supervision, Observation, and Evaluation Program: What You Can Expect and How You Can Succeed

Month 5: Understanding and Using Data: Testing/Assessment and Other Research

Month 6: Lesson Planning, Instructional Delivery, and Classroom Management

Month 7: Observing Students: Connecting What You See With What You Do

Month 8: Differentiating Instruction and Assessment: Helping All Learners Achieve

Month 9: Statewide Testing Protocol, Practices, and Issues

Month 10: Mentor/Mentee Get Together, Celebrate, and Plan for the Coming Year

As Dan concluded his review of the strengths and highlights of the monthly meetings, he turned his attention to the materials he included in his Professional Portfolio from the "end of the school year" workshops required of all probationary educators. The first item he saw was the pamphlet of workshop offerings for that last week of school.

Conducting Professional Development
Best Practice: End-of-the-School-Year Workshops

The end of year workshops were managed by the personnel director and developed in collaboration with a team of administrators, teachers, and other educators. Issues regarding facilitators, locations, time frames, attendance, refreshments, materials, equipment, and other logistics were also managed through the Office of Personnel. The content of the workshops was directly related to student performance and district goals.

As Dan read the pamphlet describing the end-of-the-year workshop offerings, he recalled being surprised at the variety of workshops listed. He placed a checkmark against the courses he thought would be most valuable and interesting to him, and he circled the two he actually completed to fulfill district requirements and meet his own learning goals.

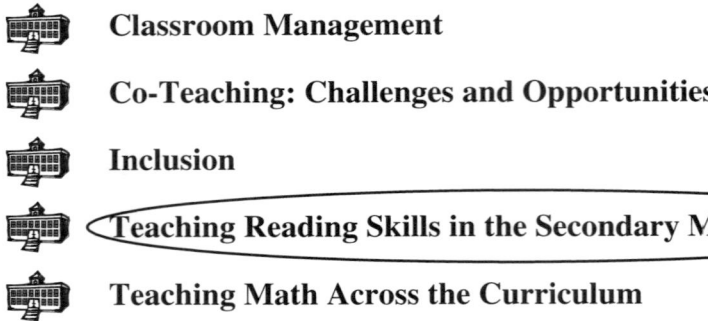

Classroom Management

Co-Teaching: Challenges and Opportunities

Inclusion

Teaching Reading Skills in the Secondary Math Curriculum

Teaching Math Across the Curriculum

Teaching Reading on the Secondary Level

Technology in the Classroom: Using PowerPoint

Technology in the Classroom: Using your PDA

He summarized his assessment of this professional development practice by listing these five major strengths:

1. The workshops were offered during the week immediately following the last day of school. This made it convenient for participants to plan the rest of their summer schedule.
2. The variety of workshops provided something valuable for everyone, even within the core curriculum.
3. The district awarded inservice credit for completing required course work.
4. All the probationary teachers could interact with each other. This was one of the few opportunities for first-year probationary educators to collaborate or learn with others who were also working toward tenure/permanence.
5. Teachers, pupil personnel and administrators from Centerville conducted most of the end-of-the-school-year workshops.

Conducting Professional Development Best Practice: Aligning Professional Development Experiences

Dan considered the strengths or areas of improvement for the professional development component and emphasized that almost all of the professional development activities he participated in were aligned with each other. For example,

- During the districtwide monthly meeting in the teacher's first month of teaching, the assistant superintendent held a session to help participants make "Meet the Teacher/Back to School Night" a success for all involved.
- During the faculty meeting that same month, the building principal and two veteran teachers provided additional helpful tips to the

whole faculty regarding the same topic, with a special focus on Meet the Teacher/Back to School Night at the high school.

- During the departmental meeting during the same month, the mathematics department chairperson also shared Meet the Teacher/Back to School Night–related strategies and materials. He focused on issues and answers specific to department policies, parent concerns, and student issues and needs.

As Dan looked through other materials from that first year of orientation, he observed the same pattern of alignment and connectedness.

This district's careful alignment of professional development experiences helped him use the knowledge and skills he was expected to demonstrate within and beyond his classroom. He concluded that a fourth major strength of the professional development component of Building Block 3: Orienting was the purposeful alignment of learning experiences for new educators. He next moved to the first workshop session of his summer orientation.

During that first morning session, the personnel director introduced the new educators to Centerville's Professional Portfolio (Figure 3.1) expectations. She advised them that they would find that their portfolios would give them many opportunities to reflect on and respond to best educational practices throughout their careers. "How right she was!" Dan thought as he gathered the materials to complete the assessment of the mentor/mentee component of Building Block 3.

MENTORING AND COLLABORATING ■

Since mentoring involved Dan and his mentor, Dan asked his mentor if he would help him assess this part of the induction initiative. The mentor agreed to meet with Dan during their common planning time. Dan recalled being especially pleased to see his mentor at the summer orientation program, where he learned they were paired for mentoring. The mentor had been a member of the interview committee that recommended his appointment to the math position. According to Dan's copy of the agenda for the summer orientation program (Figure 3.3) he had completed three years ago, the assistant superintendent and teacher association president co-led the "Introduction to Mentoring" part of the orientation. They opened the workshop with an icebreaker so each mentor/mentee pair could get to know each other. The participants were encouraged to interview each other by asking a few simple questions about

- Professional and educational experiences
- Favorite things
- Family fun

Following that getting-to-know-each-other exercise, they completed a series of formal activities designed to help them fulfill their roles as mentors and mentees.

Figure 3.4   Characteristics of Centerville School District Mentoring Program

Research-based
Organized to retain new and master educators
Aligned with the districtwide programs of professional development and
     supervision, observation and evaluation (Figure 2.8)
Designed to help new and veteran members of the Centerville school
     community connect with each other and the district
Structured to create a master teacher corps

Roles, Responsibilities, and Training
for Mentors and Mentees

In this district, all mentors are volunteers who are selected on the basis of their expertise at helping other educators use best practices. Mentors are given inservice credit, a stipend, or a reduced assignment for their work. Occasionally they are funded to attend a conference. Since the mentor and mentee were together for three years, getting to know a bit about each other is important. Dan and his mentor agreed that one of the best features of the mentoring program was the fact that all the mentor-mentee pairs participated in that summer orientation workshop where the assistant superintendent and the teacher association president emphasized the purpose of Centerville's mentoring approach.

Dan reminded his mentor of the acronym, "ROADS." The outline established that all Centerville practices were intended to help the members of the district fulfill their mission (Figure 1.1) and achieve their shared purpose (Figure 1.2). In that context, the outline used the acronym ROADS to describe the characteristics of Centerville's mentoring program (se Figure 3.4).

After a short discussion, Dan and his mentor agreed that the assessment should include one example of the first three characteristics of the mentoring program.

Mentoring Best Practice: Research-Based

Dan was one of the first teachers to suggest that the district should consider a mentoring program as part of the comprehensive approach to induction. He collaborated with a team of administrators and other educators in an action research project to gather information and prepare a report indicating best practices in mentoring. He said that the research process made him more informed and confident about mentoring.

"The team actually broke up into a few small groups. We paired off to visit five different local school districts using a variety of mentoring models. After the first round of visits and intense discussion about the pros and cons of each district, a core group of us returned to two districts for a more intensive look at their programs. We visited a few places on the web and looked at three recent articles on mentoring. The mentors and mentees from successful programs told us that they felt connected to their district through mentoring, and our research showed that people who feel a personal connection to their place of work are more likely to stay there."[2]

Figure 3.5 Features of a Multi-Modal Mentoring Program

1. Mentors must:
   a. Complete a mentor academy professional development program
   b. Apply to the personnel director to become mentors

2. Mentors can be:
   a. Current members of the professional staff
   b. Retirees
   c. Consultants

3. Mentors can be compensated by:
   a. Inservice credit
   b. Stipend
   c. One fewer period of teaching or duty assignment

4. Mentees can be supported by:
   a. A professional development program helping them understand the role of the mentees
   b. One fewer period of teaching or duty assignment

5. Mentees can be:
   a. Any probationary educator
   b. Any educator who needs help and accepts mentoring

6. Mentors and Mentees can:
   a. Share a common planning period
   b. Use other mutually agreeable meeting and communication strategies

7. Mentors and Mentees can:
   a. Observe each other or visit colleagues' classes together
   b. Attend conferences or courses together

The mentor continued, "After reviewing a variety of mentoring models,[3,4] we felt that one size could not fit every need. The model selected should be based on the goals and needs of the building or even the department. Our goals and needs were based on our student performance. Therefore every department and building can have a different set of goals and needs. For example, the whole high school had to address new graduation requirements and state assessments. The math department had to set goals and address needs related to a complete change in the state standards and core curriculum. The secondary schools had different scheduling constraints and opportunities than the elementary programs. That's why we recommended and the district adopted a multi-modal mentoring program."

The mentor proceeded to show Dan the outline (Figure 3.5) his team prepared illustrating the hallmarks of a multi-modal mentoring program.

Mentoring Best Practice:
Organized to Retain New and Master Educators

"We are living proof that the mentoring program helps new and master educators remain in a district," said Dan. "I might have explored the option of going to another district that had a slightly higher salary schedule, but I really felt connected and supported here."

"You're right" the mentor said to Dan. " I might have explored other opportunities outside this school district, too. Math teachers are in demand. It was good to have the chance to stay involved in math education in a whole different way. I had no idea I would learn as much from mentoring as you think you learned from me."

They agreed to report that the mentoring process directly affected their commitment to the district. Other mentor/mentee pairs around the district had shared similar feelings during workshops and meetings over the previous three years. Centerville's mentor program had proven so successful that periodic evaluation indicated that many teachers had already planned to serve as mentors after they retired. This was another indicator that the district was meeting its recruitment and retention goals with probationary and tenured staff.[5]

Mentoring Best Practice: Mentoring Is Aligned
With Other Professional Development Goals and Practices

Since the mentor had spent the previous ten years working in Centerville, his perspective on the induction initiative was different from his mentee's. Before instituting the induction initiative, Centerville School District approached each professional development goal or practice as a separate entity. For example, a conference day might focus on a statewide and district-level initiative, such as school safety and codes of conduct. It did not always occur to the participants in the mentoring program that the mentors could help the mentees explore how to use the learning presented during the conference day. In fact, surveys showed that mentors and mentees rarely discussed or explored the topics presented during conference days or other professional development programs.

The induction initiative motivated Centerville's educators to organize a Professional Development Committee. The purpose of the committee was to align all professional development activities with district goals. Their first step was to gather data. They used surveys, observations, and other sources to establish professional development goals and needs based on (a) student performance data in specific learning and safety areas and (b) best practices for helping adults learn.

Specifically, Centerville's data mining process indicated that

- Students across grade levels needed to develop specific reading and study skills
- Teachers across grade levels used learner objectives, questioning techniques, and closure inconsistently and sometimes incorrectly
- Parents wanted to know how they could help their children succeed in school, at home, and in the community

As a result of the committee's work, conference days, workshops, mentoring, seminars, job-embedded professional development, staff meetings, departmental meetings, and grade-level meetings all included learning experiences regarding these same topics. Mentors and mentees then focused on using the same learning in a variety of contexts. Many teams used the same professional development activity evaluation form (Figure 3.6) to monitor and assess their own collaboration on a regular basis. This made the mentor/mentee experience more meaningful to the participants and more consistent with the district goals.

As Dan and his mentor concluded their overview of best practices for mentoring, Dan turned to the section of his Professional Portfolio where he kept his observations and evaluations. "This will be the last section of my report to the committee," he observed. "Looking back, I can see how my professional development activities impacted my teaching and my students' learning. This district always drew a direct line from student learning to my own teaching and learning. The preorientation program, then orientation, then the monthly meetings, the workshops for probationary teachers, and mentoring activities all helped me see how my teaching and learning impact my students' learning and safety. At a monthly meeting about evaluation, my principal used this graphic (Figure 3.7) to explain how the district's supervision, observation, and evaluation practices are also designed to impact our students' learning and safety."

SUPERVISING, OBSERVING, AND EVALUATING ■

Supervision Best Practice: Fostering a Partnership Between a Supervisor and Another Educator

Centerville School District defined "supervision" as a set of formal and informal activities designed to:

- Support standards of excellence
- Inform best practices
- Foster partnerships between supervisors, such as principals, and other educators, primarily teachers but also other staff members
- Nurture educators
- Create opportunities to recognize and promote educators for using best practices
- Function as a master educator[6]

This definition was included in a cover sheet the assistant principal gave Dan following their first conversation during his first week of school, three years ago. He kept the paperwork from that conversation because he felt she helped him improve his instructional delivery, classroom management, and discipline in a series of recommendations and conversations about teaching. Dan decided to include "informal supervision" as one of Centerville's best practices, since he significantly improved his teaching practices and classroom management as a result of early and informal supervision.

Figure 3.6 Evaluation Form for Professional Development Activities

Directions: Please circle the most appropriate response for each item.	1 Excellent	2 Good	3 Satisfactory	4 Poor	5 Not Applicable
Connection to Standards of Professional Practice (Figure 2.6)					
Content areas/standards	1	2	3	4	5
Instructional delivery	1	2	3	4	5
Classroom management/discipline	1	2	3	4	5
Knowledge of student characteristics and needs	1	2	3	4	5
Planning and preparation	1	2	3	4	5
Collaboration	1	2	3	4	5
Reflective/responsive practices	1	2	3	4	5
Evaluation/assessment of student learning	1	2	3	4	5
Professional conduct and demeanor	1	2	3	4	5
Scheduling	1	2	3	4	5
Location	1	2	3	4	5
Usefulness	1	2	3	4	5
Presentation strategies	1	2	3	4	5
Activities for participants	1	2	3	4	5
Materials	1	2	3	4	5
What I expected from this professional development activity:	What I learned or received in this professional development activity:				
How I will apply what I learned or received in this professional development activity:	I would like more information/ assistance about:				

Figure 3.7 Promoting Student Learning and Safety

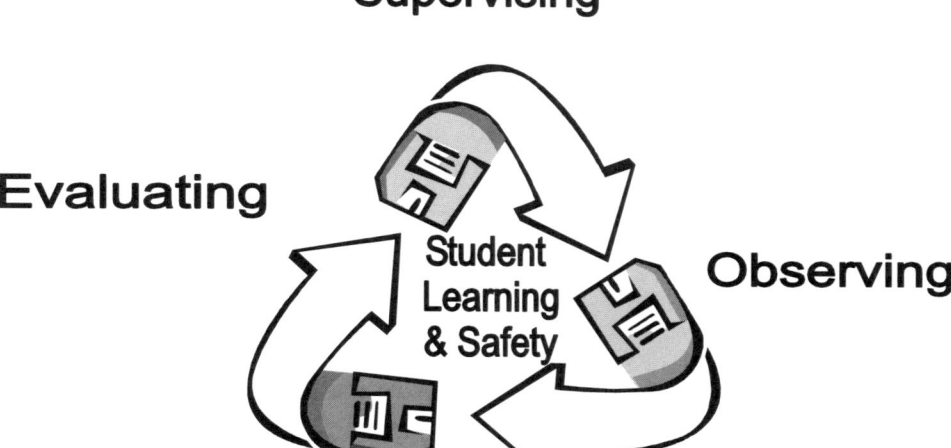

Informal Supervision

Like many other teachers still new to the profession, Dan remembered certain things from his first year as if they had just taken place. He recalled how he had just released his class about a minute or two after the bell rang, and he was feeling especially frustrated. He felt that some of his classes were finding it too difficult to focus, and he was beginning to wonder if he might have made a bad career choice when he decided to become a teacher. This did not feel the same as student teaching. At that particular moment the assistant principal stopped by his door and asked if he had a few minutes for a quick conversation. Since it was a preparatory period, he had the time, so he welcomed her into the classroom. The assistant principal asked him how things were going in his first weeks, and he recalled being somewhat defensive. Dan remembered making comments designed to assure his supervisor that he was okay.

The assistant principal responded by confiding that many of the new teachers were actually feeling a little overwhelmed, and if he should feel that way she hoped Dan would connect with her or anyone else he might trust to help him. Then she went on to say that over a few days she had noticed that Dan was releasing this period class a little after the bell rang. That meant his students were in the halls after the bell, stopping at lockers and arriving late at their next classes. She wondered if there was anything she might do to help him end the class on time.

Dan recalled that he remained a little reserved at first and then said he could use a suggestion. The assistant principal shared how some teachers would start class at the bell with a "Do Now" and end class about three or four minutes before the bell with a regularly scheduled "Closure." They would then ask students to take the last minute of class to check assignments, clean up around them, quietly pack, and exit as the bell rang. She wondered if he and his students might feel more focused and organized if he tried a version of that approach.

Dan decided to observe a colleague using the technique the assistant principal recommended. On the basis of that observation, he adapted the strategies to meet his own needs. As a result of that early experience, he felt more confident about:

- His ability to teach
- His supervisor's role as a source of practical support

Dan chose to highlight an instance of formal supervision to help the Induction Task Force understand how his success was directly related to Centerville's program of supervision, observation, and evaluation.

Formal Observation

During his first observation, he recalled at least three things going wrong from the outset. The students did not seem to recall much of what he thought would require only a brief review. The maintenance person mowed the lawn outside his window, and the bulb blew out in the overhead projector he was using, which caused the students to laugh. In his postobservation session, he expected his principal to criticize him extensively for what he perceived to be these errors. Instead, the high school principal praised him for

- Adapting his lesson to meet the needs of his students
- Briefly using appropriate humor to acknowledge the lawn mowing and the overhead projector problem, then quickly refocusing students on the lesson

He did not expect the high school principal to ask him the question that he now asks himself every day: "If you were a physical education teacher, when would your students get the ball during the lesson? If you taught music, when would the students get to sing or play an instrument during the lesson?"

He was astonished at the question, and did not know how to answer it. The principal explained that he wanted Dan to use every appropriate strategy to make sure the students were actively engaged in learning for the most number of minutes possible. As a result of that dialogue,[7] Dan observed music and physical education teachers, eventually took several courses about instructional strategies to increase meaningful student engagement in learning, and was able to show his progress over subsequent observations.

PUTTING IT TOGETHER FOR THE INDUCTION TASK FORCE

As Dan reviewed his materials one last time before presenting them to the Induction Task Force, he considered how Centerville's programs for professional development and for supervision, observation and evaluation had helped him:

- Remain a teacher
- Stay in Centerville
- Recruit friends to teach at Centerville
- Look forward to fulfilling new roles in his capacity as a tenured professional member of the Centerville learning community

CHAPTER SUMMARY ■

This chapter was designed to serve as a resource you can use to develop a year-long orientation program for first-year staff members. The orientation program described in this chapter included three major strands that you can use to help your first-year staff members connect with the school, the district, and community; guide first-year staff to follow school and district policies, practices, and procedures; and align orientation with the school and district programs for professional development and supervision, observation, and evaluation.

Tips

Connections

- Update your preorientation packet to ensure accurate names, numbers, and so forth
- (And **Professional Development**) Encourage school and district educators to facilitate professional development programs within the district, either:
  - In collaboration with colleges/universities, or
  - As part of the inservice education program
- (And **Professional Development**) Pair mentors and mentees based on:
  - The mentor's proficiency in instructional delivery, classroom management, collaboration with students, parents and other educators, and other standards of professional practice (See Figure 2.6: Nine Standards of Professional Practice)
  - The mentee's strengths and needs
- Encourage department chairpersons to support the ongoing mentor/mentee relationship

Data Mining

Profile your newly hired staff for such characteristics as
- Preservice education
- Previous experience
- Graduate degrees and other certificates
- Major areas of study

Example: An elementary teacher may also have completed training in a special reading approach or minored in science. You may choose to use that information in placing that elementary teacher.

Finance

- (And **Data Mining**) Anticipate and incorporate the budgetary and other finance-related implications of a mentoring program, including such factors as release time, stipends for mentors/mentees, inservice credit, and other related issues.
- Fully fund your orientation program.

Legal Issues

- (And **Personnel Issues**) Publicize your tenure/permanence process to all staff members. Help all stakeholders understand that tenure/permanence:
  - Is a major event in an educator's career
  - Expresses the district's conclusion that this qualified educator has made a commitment and connection to the school, district, and profession

Personnel Issues

- Include members of the teachers association and other best-qualified staff in developing, implementing, and annually updating the orientation program.
- Encourage mentors and mentees to participate in shared professional development activities, especially during conference days and other programs conducted within the school day.

Professional Development

- Use your faculty and departmental meetings as opportunities to:
  - Model good instructional techniques
  - Engage in formal professional development

    Example: Involve educators in viewing a videotape of instructional delivery, follow district guidelines to complete an observation of that lesson, and compare and contrast results to promote shared language and shared standards of excellence.

- Use faculty, departmental- and grade-level meetings, observations, and evaluations as opportunities to:
  - Disseminate and use a "shared vocabulary" for professional practices that are observed and evaluated

■ NOTES

1. Preorientation is a period of time between the hiring of the educator and the beginning of the summer orientation program.

2. Buckingham, M, & Coffman, C. (1999). *First break all the rules: What the world's greatest managers do differently.* New York: Simon & Schuster.

3. Podsen, I., & Denmark, V. (2000). *Coaching and mentoring first-year and student teachers.* New York: Eye on Education.

4. Darling-Hammond, L. (1998). Teacher learning that supports student learning. *Educational Leadership, 55*(5), 6-11.

5. Anderson, G., Herr, K., & Nihlen, A. (1994). *Studying your own school.* Thousand Oaks, CA: Corwin, 156.

6. Nadeau, A. & Leighton, M. (1996). *The role of leadership in sustaining school reform: Voices from the field.* Washington, DC: U.S. Department of Education.

7. Vella, J. (1995). *Training through dialogue: Promoting effective learning and change with adults.* San Francisco: Jossey-Bass.

BLUEPRINT FOR BUILDING BLOCK 3

	GOALS	PARTICIPANTS	OBJECTIVES	NEXT STEPS
Building Block 3	*Orienting*			
	Preorientation			
3a	• Develop procedures to help new educators "connect" with district/building/ department/grades • Create core curriculum • Align supervision, observation, and evaluation with the core curriculum for new educators	• Personnel director • Building principals • Department chairs • Teacher Association • Other educators	Objectives: • Use data to develop **what** all new educators should know and do • Use data to decide **how** to implement a comprehensive induction program	Implement, monitor, assess, and refine the content and procedures that are part of "connecting" the new educator to the Centerville school community
3b	When new educators are hired, implement preorienting activities	• School/community leaders • Personnel director • Newly hired educators	The personnel director ensures that all newly hired educators receive necessary materials and schedules	Personnel director surveys the newly hired educators and others involved to evaluate the reaching out process

	GOALS	PARTICIPANTS	OBJECTIVES	NEXT STEPS
	Orientation			
_3c	Implement a districtwide orientation program	Key members of the district facilitate the orientation session	• Continue building and strengthening connections between and among members of the district • Provide opportunities for participants to earn credits or receive other kinds of compensation consistent with district policy • Help newly hired educators develop the shared language and goals of the Centerville school community	Personnel director uses the information, shares the results, and collaborates with other leaders to refine the orientation program
_3d	Implement building-level orientation programs	• Each newly hired educator • Building-level administrators • Lead teachers • Districtwide staff, when appropriate, including pupil personnel and department chairs • Personnel director	Formal: • Principal/AP invites newly hired educators to specific programs Informal: • New/veteran staff meet, share ideas; newly hired educator reports to the office and visits; may set up classroom for the year • Strengthen connections, make newly hired educators and veterans feel welcome and secure	• Sustain culture of collaboration and mutual support • Create formal, schedule-based opportunities for staff members to collaborate

(Continued)

BLUEPRINT FOR BUILDING BLOCK 3 *(Continued)*

	GOALS	PARTICIPANTS	OBJECTIVES	NEXT STEPS
	Professional Development			
_3e	Conduct monthly districtwide professional development programs for newly hired educators	• All newly hired educators • Administrators • Department chairs • Lead teachers • Consultants	• Ensure that professional development programs advance the learning and safety goals of the district • Choose professional development subjects on the basis of ongoing data mining	• Create, monitor, and assess impact of the professional development plan (PDP) of each new educator • Establish mentor-mentee relationships based on data indicating strengths and needs of each
_3f	Use data to plan and implement end of school year	All probationary educators	Ensure that topics of the professional development programs advance the learning and safety goals of the district	Refine, evaluate, and report on progress of professional development
	Mentoring/Collaborating			
_3g	Research mentoring models	• Administrators • Teachers • University staff • Consultants	Propose one or more mentoring and collaboration models so each new teacher is formally connected with at least one other educator who can fulfill the role of mentor during at least one academic year	Ensure mentoring models are appropriately differentiated to meet district, student, and staff needs

	GOALS	PARTICIPANTS	OBJECTIVES	NEXT STEPS
__3h	Implement and sustain the mentoring practices	• Mentors-mentees • Building administrators • Teacher Association leaders	Connect newly hired educators with tenured/permanent members of the staff	Regularly evaluate progress and adjust accordingly
	Supervising, Observing, and Evaluating			

__3i	Develop a program that helps the district:
	  • Meet learning and safety goals
	  • Attract and retain the best educators for the district
	  • Ensure use of best practices
		• Administrators
		• Teacher Association members
		• Veteran teachers
		• Department chairs
		• Newly tenured teachers
		• Newly hired educators
		• Retirees
		• Consultants
			Pilot the program	• Evaluate the program
				• Evaluate the individual practices of the staff members involved
				• Make appropriate staffing decisions
				• Make appropriate changes in the program

__3j	Implement the districtwide program of supervision, observation, and evaluation	• All probationary educators • Administrators • Department chairs • Lead teachers • Consultants	• Conduct at least four formal evaluations per probationary year • Evaluate educator performance in regard to district/building-level goals	Use the data to: • Establish professional development topics and goals for the end-of-school-year Probationary Educators' Workshops • Identify newly hired educators in need of additional support • Provide appropriate support • Evaluate progress • Make appropriate staffing decisions

4

Creating Lasting Connections for Your Probationary Professional Staff

Years Two and Three

THIS CHAPTER WILL HELP YOU

- Continue to connect probationary staff with your school and district
- Use data mining and other best practices to make decisions regarding the performance of probationary staff
- Enhance instructional delivery and other practices for probationary staff
- Follow a tenure/permanence process to retain the best qualified staff

Amy Pierce spent the first ten years of her career working as an accountant. Since Amy had always loved working with children, she responded to a Centerville School District recruitment campaign targeting professionals interested in making midcareer changes. After one meeting with Personnel Director Stephanie Blair, and a small group of Centerville teachers who made similar career changes, Amy decided to take the "career ladder" approach to becoming a teacher. As a result, after Amy completed her certification in elementary education, Centerville offered her a position as a fourth grade teacher.

The Induction Task Force recently asked Amy to share her assessment of Building Block 4 from the point of view of a probationary teacher. Since she had just been awarded tenure, her second and third years of probationary practice were still fresh in her memory. Since she had just completed an inservice technology course designed to help her sharpen her PowerPoint skills, Amy decided to use PowerPoint in her presentation to the Induction Task Force. This chapter details how she organized her presentation to include the essential elements of Building Block 4.

Amy reviewed the Benchmarks for Building Block 4 (Figure 4.1) that she placed in her Professional Portfolio at the beginning of her second year at Centerville. As she scanned the items she was selecting for her report to the Induction Task Force, she realized how she and her other newly tenured colleagues had particularly benefited from the three areas below:

- Professional development
- Supervision, observation and evaluation
- Granting tenure/permanence

She believed that these examples would illustrate how Centerville helps probationary teachers establish enduring connections to the district.

She divided "Ongoing Professional Development" and "Supervision, Observation and Evaluation" into two categories: "Formal" and "Informal." In this way, she illustrated how these practices:

- Aligned with each other
- Met district, building, grade level, or subject area goals
- Were promoted by administrators, teachers, and other educators

Since adopting the Building Blocks, Centerville School District defined formal practices as usually

- Specific to participants' roles
- Scheduled
- Formally measured
- Part of the official record

Figure 4.1 Benchmarks for Building Block 4: Connecting

	Ongoing Professional Development Activities	Formal Observations Required	Informal Evaluations	Mid-Year Evaluation	End of School Year Workshops	End of Year Evaluation	Tenure/Permanence
Year Two BB 4: Connecting (Total 30 hours of formal professional development)	Formal: 15 hours of activities approved by the principal/curriculum supervisor. Based on data from student performance and observations/evaluations of professional staff	4 (minimum) conducted by the principal/other supervisor	Ongoing	Completed by the principal/other supervisor. Includes portfolio review	Formal: 15 hours of activities initiated and provided by the district	Completed by the principal/other supervisor	
Year Three BB 4: Connecting (Total 30 hours of	Formal: 15 hours of activities approved by the	4 (minimum) conducted by the principal/other supervisor	Ongoing	Completed by the principal/other supervisor. Includes	Formal: 15 hours of activities initiated and provided by the district	Completed by the principal/other supervisor	1. Recommended by principal/supervisor to superintendent

(Continued)

Figure 4.1 *(Continued)*

formal professional development	principal/curriculum supervisor Based on data from student performance and observations/ evaluations of professional staff		portfolio review		2. Recommended by superintendent to board of education

Figure 4.2 PowerPoint Slide: Title Page—Highlights From the Report to the Induction Task Force

---

Report to the Induction Task Force
Centerville School District

Induction:
Connecting Recruitment to Retention

Focus On:
Building Block 4: Connecting

Prepared by
Amy Pierce

Teacher, Grade 4, Centerville Elementary School

Examples of formal practices typically included:

- Formal observations by administrators and supervisors
- Courses, workshops, and seminars
- Annual professional performance evaluations
- Professional improvement plans

The district defined informal practices as usually:

- Related more to participants' expertise than roles
- Impromptu; scheduled on the basis of participants' priorities
- Informally measured
- Not part of the official record

Examples of informal practices could include:

- Teachers sharing instructional strategies during a mutually convenient time during or after school
- Peer observations between or among teachers, administrators, pupil personnel, and others
- Informal observation of instruction by an administrator
- District-based electronic bulletin board information-sharing about standards, assessments, student development, and so forth

Amy's recent experience in a technology course was a good example of how Centerville promoted formal and informal professional development. At the formal level, she enrolled in the course because it helped her meet professional goals and provided her with inservice credit. At the informal level, the instructor encouraged students to seek out any member of the professional staff who could help them use their new learning in practical ways. He wanted to emphasize that this kind of effort was part of the district's culture of professional development.

Figure 4.3 PowerPoint Slide: Table of Contents—From the Report to the Induction Task Force

---

Table of Contents

Ongoing Professional Development
Formal
Informal

Ongoing Supervision, Observation, & Evaluation
Formal
Informal

Granting Tenure/Permanence
Formal

During the course, Amy asked her technology instructor to recommend a teacher from her building who could help her transfer her new learning into everyday practice. He suggested several people, including the principal, a teacher in her building, and her mentor. With the help of her principal, Amy observed a colleague using the same technology to help fourth-grade students learn. Then she met with her mentor for help integrating technology into her instructional and assessment activities more consistently and appropriately, given the characteristics of her students.

As she organized her materials for her Building Block 4 report, Amy reflected on how her current district compared with the school where she had student-taught. She had participated in a similar technology workshop during the first month of student teaching, but never actually used what she learned in that course. There had been no support system to help her apply the new learning in practical ways in her own instructional setting. In fact, many educators in the building where she student-taught questioned the value of integrating technology into their everyday practices.

Once Amy decided how to represent the informal and formal aspects of professional development, supervision, and observation, she focused on highlighting the three best practices for professional development indicated in Figure 4.4 below.

ONGOING PROFESSIONAL DEVELOPMENT BEST PRACTICE: DATA MINING

Amy chose data mining[1] as an example of a best practice of formal, ongoing professional development. From the district's wide variety of data-mining activities, she focused on the Survey of Professional Development and Teacher Practices (Figure 4.5). It was the first survey she participated in as

Figure 4.4 PowerPoint Slide

**Best Practices:
Ongoing Professional
Development**

1. Formal

   - Used data mining to design, implement, and evaluate professional development activities
   - Provided a core curriculum as part of professional development for all probationary educators through Building Blocks 3 and 4

2. Informal

   - Helped educators informally work together across and within grade levels, buildings, and subject areas

---

a second-year teacher, and it was the first time she saw the connections among survey results, professional development practices and student learning. For example, as a result of the survey, the core curriculum for probationary teachers was changed to reflect the district's goals as well as the newly identified needs and strengths of students and staff.

The survey (Figure 4.5) was designed to discover:

- Instructional strategies teachers customarily use
- The teacher's comfort level in using these strategies
- Where and how the teacher learned the strategy
- What teachers believe students should be doing while teachers are using the strategy

Amy liked the way the survey results were used in a variety of formal and informal ways around the district. On the formal level, the district Professional Development Committee used the results to redesign and update the core curriculum for all professional staff.

On the informal level, individuals who participated in the survey used the results to reflect on their own practices. After the nontenured teachers completed the survey, they were invited to participate in an inservice course in which they discussed specific techniques they used or wanted to use. They discussed how some of the items on the survey could be used in the classroom to support instruction. The initial course allowed the instructor and participants to plan for future staff development that would focus more specifically on selected techniques of interest to the teachers. In both the initial and future courses the goals were the same:

- Determine the appropriate techniques to achieve instructional goals.
- Align the techniques with district goals.

Figure 4.5 Survey of Professional Development and Teacher Practices

A	*Strategy* *Circle the number to indicate the strategies you use. Use the columns to the right to indicate your comfort scale and source for the strategies you circled.*	*Comfort Scale* *1 = Expert* *2 = Competent* *3 = Novice*	*Source* *Where did you learn the most about this strategy?*
1	Authentic Assessment		
2	Brain-Based Learning		
3	Constructivism		
4	Cooperative Learning		
5	Co-Teaching		
6	Differentiated Instruction		
7	Guided Reading		
8	Integrated Reading (check the research)		
9	Learning Centers		
10	Learning Styles		
11	Leveled Texts		
12	Literacy Profiles		
13	Math Manipulatives		
14	Miscue Analysis		
15	Phonics		
16	Portfolio Assessment		
17	Reader's Workshop		
18	Rubrics		
19	Running Records		
20	Station Teaching		
21	Technology in Classroom/ Professional Practices		
22	Whole Group Instruction		
23	Whole Language		
24	Writer's Workshop		

B   Please choose two or three of the strategies you believe are the most important of those you identified in the previous list. Describe what students are doing while you are employing this strategy in your classroom.

_____

_____

_____

_____

_____

_____

C   Please describe another strategy that was not on the list and that you use regularly during classroom instruction. How confident are you in using this strategy? Where did you learn the most about this strategy?

_____

_____

_____

_____

_____

_____

SOURCE: Adapted from the "Staff Development Survey," Spring 2002, developed by David Flatley, Assistant Superintendent, Curriculum and Instruction, South Country School District, East Patchogue, New York.

Amy highlighted data mining as a best practice for professional development because it had such a direct effect on her classroom instruction. For the same reasons, she featured the district's program of supervision, observation, and evaluation.

ONGOING SUPERVISION, OBSERVATION, AND EVALUATION BEST PRACTICES: FORMAL OBSERVATION AND INFORMAL SUPERVISION

Formal Observation

In her report to the Induction Task Force, Amy circled one pivotal experience to illustrate how a formal observation became the catalyst to help her improve her instructional delivery (see Figure 4.6).

Figure 4.6 Connecting Best Practices

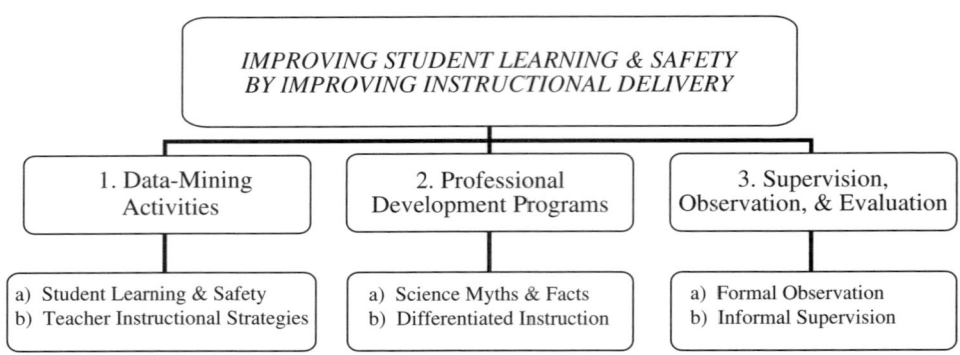

She began explaining this example by reflecting on her second and third years of teaching. During that probationary period, she used a strategy recommended to all professional staff: to use the district Evaluation Instrument (See Resource I) as a guide to best instructional practices.

Amy knew she was not expected to be perfect. Most importantly, she knew that the district's observation and evaluation instrument and processes were designed to help her continuously improve. In planning a preobservation conference with her principal, Amy wanted to demonstrate how she would use her new instructional skills to help her students:

- Achieve the intended objectives
- Use appropriate reading materials
- Complete all the primary steps of a lab activity
- Benefit from materials, activities, and strategies that were appropriately differentiated to meet the needs of all learners

During their preobservation conference, Amy and her principal clarified the learner objectives and specified how she could monitor and assess student learning. The subsequent observation and postobservation conference became a turning point for Amy. During the postobservation conference that followed Amy's lesson about scientific inquiry, her principal opened the conversation the way she always began a postobservation conference. She asked Amy to describe one strength of the lesson and one area to improve in her lesson.

Amy immediately responded that all the students were academically engaged throughout the lesson because she chose the right strategies to help the students achieve the objectives. She was satisfied that the instructional strategies she learned through her professional development survey and coursework contributed to the strengths of the lesson. Amy felt she could improve how she and her students moved from one activity or location to another but didn't know how to make that improvement.

The principal agreed with both of Amy's observations. After complimenting Amy on how accurately she assessed her own performance, she offered several suggestions. She suggested that Amy consider the following ways to build on her strengths and correct her weaknesses and to expect concrete help from her or an experienced teacher, if she preferred to work with a colleague:

- Plan transitions as elements of the lesson plan
- Pace instruction to help students achieve more in the allocated time

Before they ended the meeting, Amy's principal assured her that she was doing quite well and that having one or two areas where she needed some help was completely normal. Both Amy and her principal agreed to meet again in a few days to do some co-planning. They also agreed to think a bit about which experienced teacher could be of some help and to contact that person in the next week. All of the next steps to help Amy with transitions and pacing are informal.

Informal Supervision

Amy recalled that her principal described informal supervision as a partnership among Amy, her peers, and her supervisors. It could include collaborative lesson planning and even an opportunity for Amy to observe a teacher "model" best transitional and pacing strategies, which she did. Through informal supervision, Amy collaborated with her peers and supervisors to improve pacing and transitions by exploring:

- Steps involved
- Time factors
- Materials distribution strategies
- Assessment techniques
- Other elements of task analysis

At the first planning meeting, Amy expressed that she was concerned that all the informal suggestions might appear on her formal observation and evaluation. Her principal quickly reassured her and helped her make the distinction between formal and informal supervision and observation. She explained that the formal observation that Amy had already seen indicated that Amy applied many of the Standards of Professional Practice (Figure 2.6) in her lesson and that Amy was doing quite well generally. It also included a recommendation that Amy strengthen her transitional and pacing skills. Any informal help provided by the principal or more experienced teachers would not become part of any formal record.

Looking back at how her principal helped her distinguish between the programs of formal observation and informal supervision, Amy was convinced that these best practices helped her develop lasting connections with her principal and colleagues. From that first formal observation onward, she recalled feeling increasingly accomplished and secure with each probationary educator benchmark she completed (Figure 4.1).

ONGOING SUPERVISION, OBSERVATION, AND EVALUATION BEST PRACTICE: THE PROCESS OF GRANTING TENURE/PERMANENCE

Amy selected Centerville's tenure/permanence granting process as the final "best practice" she highlighted in her presentation to the task force. There were two elements of that process that helped her connect with the people and philosophy of the Centerville school community:

1. The portfolio review with the principal/supervisor
2. Tenure celebration for newly tenured teachers and their families

Best Practice for Granting Tenure/Permanence: The Portfolio Review With the Principal

Amy chose to highlight the portfolio review because it helped her to standardize and individualize this first step toward tenure. The portfolio review was designed to standardize the process by requiring all probationary educators and their supervisors to use the same rubric as the basis for evaluation (Figure 4.7). At the same time, the portfolio review was designed to individualize the process by ensuring that all probationary educators could select their own exemplars and testimonials. Amy understood that the portfolio review helped probationary and supervisory staff reflect on each individual's professional growth and practices over a three-year period.

Amy recalled that the portfolio review meeting with her principal followed five steps and took about forty minutes. Her principal led the discussion by reviewing Amy's:

1. Professional Portfolio
2. Observations and evaluations, with a focus on the nine standards of professional practice
3. Use of formal and informal suggestions and recommendations in her professional practices
4. "Culminating statement" expressing

    (a) The goals she set and met during her probationary period
    (b) What she planned to do to continue to improve and contribute as a member of the Centerville school community

5. Letter of recommendation from the principal to the superintendent indicating her support for Amy's tenure appointment

Amy considered the program for tenure celebration and recognition as a best practice, as well. It demonstrated that tenure/permanence was visible to, and valued by, the entire school community. Amy highlighted the tenure reception that followed the board of education meeting where she and her colleagues were formally granted tenure.

Best Practice for Granting Tenure/ Permanence: Celebration and Recognition

The tenure celebration and recognition program was collaboratively organized by the superintendent's secretary and a member of the Parent-Teacher Association, who ensured that the district:

1. Sent invitations to tenure candidates, their families, building administrators, teacher association leadership, building colleagues, and building-level Parent-Teacher Association members
2. Provided refreshments

Figure 4.7   Rubric for the Professional Portfolio: Criteria for Evaluation

CONTENT	QUALITY	EXEMPLARS	TESTIMONIALS
Includes all elements indicated in Figure 3.1 for creating and maintaining a Professional Portfolio	Completeness	Student work, such as: • Reports of student performance • Book reports, projects, etc.	Letters from supervisors
Includes at least one example of each of the Nine Standards of Professional Practice (Figure 2.6)	Neatness/ Presentation	Educator work, such as: • Selected lesson plans • Selected unit of study • A curriculum project • Assessments	Letters from parents
Demonstrates progress by • Following recommendations and suggestions; • Using new learning	Clarity	Extra/Cocurricular activities, such as: • Field trips • Coaching • Clubs • Committee work	Letters from students
Indicates benchmarks reached (Figure 4.1)	Size: Not to exceed: • A three-inch binder • A 30-slide presentation • A 10-minute video/CD	Self-Reflective Statement: "How I have helped advance Centerville School District's mission"	Letters from colleagues

3. Arranged for high school student musicians to greet those attending the program and perform during the reception
4. Ensured that a high school student photographer and the district public relations coordinator attend the celebration

Amy recalled how impressed she was to see so many representatives of the school community at the celebration. She decided to highlight this event as a best practice by adding two final slides to her PowerPoint presentation:

Figure 4.8   Best Practices: Granting Tenure/Permanence

Best Practices:
Granting Tenure/Permanence

The Invitation

Superintendent James Frasier
and the
Centerville School District Board of Education
Cordially Invite You and Your Family to Attend
A Celebration in Recognition of
Granting Tenure
May 20, 2002, at 7:30 p.m.
In the Board of Education Heritage Room

RSVP Annette Drake, Extension 555

- A copy of the invitation to the celebration (Figure 4.8)
- A copy of her tenure certificate (Figure 4.9)

■ CHAPTER SUMMARY

This chapter was designed to illustrate how your school or district can strengthen the performance of second- and third-year staff by continuing to help probationary staff connect with your school, district, and community; supporting performance of probationary staff by using data mining and programs of supervision, observation, evaluation, and professional development; following a process for granting tenure/permanence, so your school and district retains the best qualified staff.

Tips

Connections

- Award certificates of gratitude to mentors from the superintendent and board of education for their pivotal role in shaping the performance of quality teachers.
- Publish notices of teachers awarded tenure and given promotions (post on website, put in newspaper, etc.)
- (And **Professional Development**) Organize schoolwide or districtwide professional development activities so educators are grouped heterogeneously for levels of experience in the classroom.

Data Mining

- (And **Personnel Issues**) Personnel director publishes two different districtwide master charts to principals and department chairs,

Figure 4.9 Best Practices: Granting Tenure/Permanence: The Tenure Certificate

---

Best Practices:
Granting Tenure/Permanence
The Tenure Certificate

CENTERVILLE SCHOOL DISTRICT

Proudly Recognizes

Amy Pierce

On Her Tenure Appointment
as an
Elementary Educator
Dedicated to Helping All Our Children
Learn Well and Stay Safe

Dr. James Frasier   *Ms. Terry Travis*

Dr. James Frasier, Superintendent of Schools   Terry Travis, President, Board of Education

---

alphabetically listing all educators who have been observed, as well as dates and individuals who completed the observation or evaluation.

Master List 1: Alphabetical by Educator's Name

Teacher's Name	School	Date of Observation	Administrator/ Supervisor Who Observed
Smith, John	CHS Science	October 21	Hammond, A.
Taylor, Anne	CES Grade 6	December 3	Griffith, M.

Master List 2: Alphabetical by Administrator/Supervisor's Name

Administrator/Supervisor Who Observed or Evaluated the Educator	School	Date of Observation	Educator Who Was Observed
Griffith, M.	CES	December 3	Taylor, Anne
Hammond, A.	HS Science	October 21	Smith, John

Finance

- Educators' performance may be rewarded through such recognition as being encouraged or funded to present at conferences.
- (And **Connections**) Engage educators by encouraging or underwriting appropriate conference attendance, journal subscriptions, professional libraries with print, electronic and video resources, and so forth.
- Keep in mind the financial implications of how you approach all your connections, data mining, legal issues, personnel issues, and professional development.

Legal Issues

- Teacher contract and work rules: Make sure your contract and labor work rules supports your professional development and instructional goals. Where it does not, negotiate changes to give you the ability to design, implement, monitor, assess, and sustain a professional development program aligned with district learning and safety goals for students.

Personnel Issues

- (And **Data Mining**) Conduct a meta-analysis of observations and evaluations to discover areas of strengths and weaknesses in professional practice. Use this data to determine long-term and short-term opportunities and needs.

Professional Development

- (And **Connections**) Recruit staff members interested in professional development and additional course work.
- (And **Connections**) During faculty and department meetings, encourage staff to share what they have read in professional journals.
- (And **Connections**) Have a portfolio exposition where probationary teachers can share best practices for portfolio completion with their colleagues.

NOTE

1. Olson, L. (2002, June 12). Schools discovering riches in data. *Education Week.*

BLUEPRINT FOR BUILDING BLOCK 4

	GOALS	PARTICIPANTS	OBJECTIVES	NEXT STEPS
Building Block 4	Connecting	**For the Probationary Educators' Second and Third Year**		
	Professional Development			
__**4a**	Ongoing professional development • Formal: 15 hours • Approved by the principal/supervisor	All probationary second- and third-year teachers • Total of 30 hours of formal professional development	• Train and retain the best educators for Centerville School District • Implement an approach to professional development that celebrates the strengths of the staff as professional development trainers who work collaboratively with probationary educators • Nurture new educators through ongoing professional development	Help newly hired educators use best practices associated with helping all students achieve academic and safety goals

(Continued)

BLUEPRINT FOR BUILDING BLOCK 4 *(Continued)*

	GOALS	PARTICIPANTS	OBJECTIVES	NEXT STEPS
	Supervising, Observing, and Evaluating			
___ **4b**	Developing lasting connections with administrators, colleagues, and students through formal as well as informal supervision, observation, and evaluation	Principal, curriculum supervisors, probationary teachers	• Develop a "team" culture of supervision, observation, and evaluation to celebrate best practices for supervising, teaching, and learning • Use formal and informal observation to connect probationary staff with others in the effort to meet/exceed benchmarks established by the district and state	• Continue to develop/celebrate best teaching practices that reflect the district's standards of professional practice • Data mine the impact of observation/supervision/evaluation of best teaching practices on student achievement
	Granting Tenure/ Permanence			
___ **4c**	Superintendent recommends to the board of education that the identified probationary educators be granted permanent status/tenure	• Superintendent • Board of education • Administrators • Probationary teachers	• Retaining the best educators for Centerville School District • Implement a tenure celebration tradition • Continue to nurture newly permanent/tenured educators	Help newly permanent, tenured educators consistently use standards of professional practice to make decisions and select practices

5

Retaining Your High-Quality Professional Staff

Best Practices

THIS CHAPTER WILL HELP YOU

- Retain the connections you forged through Building Blocks 1–4
- Support tenured and permanent staff through your observation and evaluation practices
- Renew and reorient tenured/permanent staff
- Use data mining to plan professional development and staffing
- Ensure that professional development is responsive to tenured/permanent teacher strengths and needs

Richard Lane, a ninth-year Spanish teacher, was printing the final draft of the Centerville "Building Block 5: Retaining" Activity Guide (Figures 5.1 and 5.2) that he would help distribute to all staff on the opening day of school. His colleagues would post it on the district's website. He planned to use the same guide in his report to the Induction Task Force. Richard had recently declined another attractive position from a neighboring district, so he was especially suited to explain how Centerville's Building Block 5 initiative helped him remain connected to the school community that had become his "home."

After reflecting on which factors helped him remain a member of Centerville's faculty, Richard decided on three factors he would highlight for his presentation to the Induction Task Force.

First, he would cite the Building Block 5 Activity Guide (Figures 5.1 and 5.2), which included most of the reasons he and his colleagues continued as members of the Centerville professional community. Second, he would highlight two features of the supervision, observation, and evaluation program: these two features would be (a) that his observations continue to help him improve his instructional delivery and understanding of his students and (b) that the evaluation process helped him demonstrate how he used his observations and his professional development to improve student learning and safety. Third, he would illustrate Centerville's professional development initiative for tenured educators called the "Five Year Cycle of Renewing and Reorienting." He felt confident that the members of the Induction Task Force would understand and identify with the reasons he chose.

To illustrate to the task force how the fifth Building Block helped him establish strong connections with other staff around the district during his first year as a tenured teacher, the Spanish teacher decided to use his "Hole in One" certificate awarded by the members of the district's faculty golf club. As a member of the original subcommittee on Building Block 5: Retaining, Richard had participated in the data-mining activities that helped Centerville understand what motivated tenured, successful staff members to remain in the district. Their research[1] helped them discover at least three factors that helped staff members (a) remain in the district and (b) continuously improve their own professional performance and practices. These three factors were

1. Challenging, meaningful work
2. Rewarding friendships and other relationships with members of the school district
3. Fair compensation, benefits, recognition, and other incentives

The friendships and camaraderie he developed from the golf club and other informal groups listed in the Building Block 5 Activity Guide extended to his working relationships in his own building and throughout the district. He wanted the members of the Induction Task Force to know how he continues to build and value connections in his professional and personal life. He decided to add that he rejected offers from other districts in part because of the importance of these connections.

Another reason he continued to teach in Centerville was the on-site Graduate Extension Program where he could take university courses that were:

Figure 5.1   Retaining Best Practice: The Building Block 5 Activity Guide: Retaining the Connection

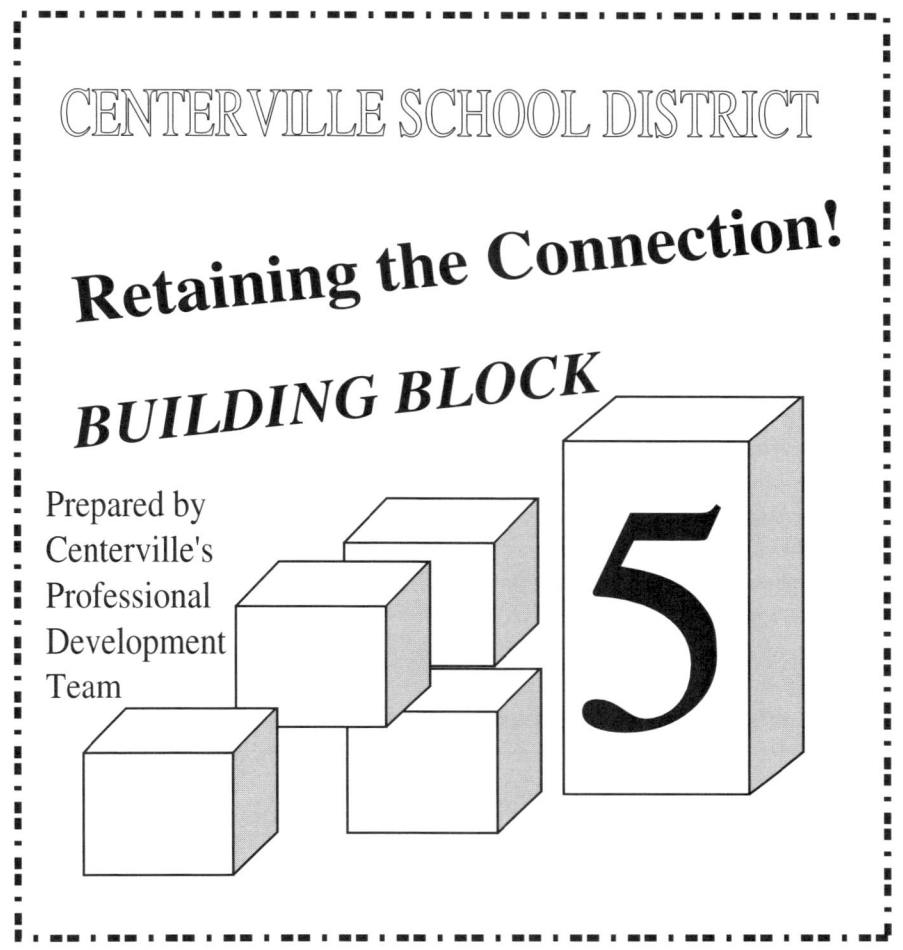

- In his building or at a nearby location
- Often taught or co-taught by in-district faculty
- Related to issues important to him and his district
- Offered at a reduced rate, in cooperation with the local university

He illustrated this highlight by referring to the course he was currently completing, titled "Differentiating Instruction for Today's Learners."

RETAINING BEST PRACTICE: OBSERVATION AND EVALUATION FOR TENURED STAFF

During the previous spring semester, Richard's supervisor had noticed some trends in classroom practices as he completed his annual evaluations

Figure 5.2 Table of Contents: Retaining the Connection Activity Guide: Building Block 5

TOPICS

Mission Statement
Welcome
Message from the Superintendent
Message from the President, Board of Education
Message from the President, Centerville Teachers
    Association
What's New in Centerville?
    Instructional
    Noninstructional
    Community
Calendar
    Districtwide Activities
    Building-Based Activities
    Special Events
    Faculty Happenings
    Regular Meetings: Clubs and Teams
    Birthday Celebrations
    Dates to Remember
    Educator Exchange Programs
Undergraduate (Career Ladder) Offerings
Graduate Offerings on Campus
In-District Grants
    Criteria
    Applications
Mentoring Updates
    Applications
    Networks
    Timelines
Faculty Publications
Websites: Staff Members
Recommended Websites

---

of each staff member. On the "strengths" side, teachers were consistently and correctly integrating technology into their instructional practices. On the "areas for improvement" side, he observed that many teachers tended to use just one or two instructional strategies. At the same time, student performance in his department was slightly below expectations as measured by state exams. The consensus of the language department was that teachers could improve student performance by using instructional practices that engaged their learners more consistently. One of the practices recommended to improve student performance was differentiating instruction.[2]

Since the "Differentiating Instruction" course was being co-taught by a principal and an experienced teacher, Richard knew that the strategies he learned would be valued and evaluated in the practical setting of his Spanish class. He and several other veteran members of his department decided to take this course together for the following reasons:

(a) They were feeling frustrated because the state and district had begun to require all students in the district to complete a unit of language other than English in order to graduate. This was a change in policy. Like many of their colleagues in other departments, they were accustomed to teaching students who had selected the course and were highly motivated to learn the content. He and many of his colleagues found the range of new learners challenging.

(b) The course was offered on-site, at a convenient time.

(c) Other Centerville educators who had completed and evaluated the course found it hands-on, practical, and worthwhile.

(d) Their department chairperson recommended that they take the course.

Richard decided to use this example of the connection between observation and evaluation as another reason why he remained a member of the Centerville school community. He felt challenged, respected, and supported in his ongoing effort to meet the changing needs of his students and his district. Since Centerville had prepared him to anticipate that the entire staff would always need to continuously improve their practices, he never felt disrespected or threatened when a supervisor recommended that he improve his instructional practices. He understood that this was part of the Centerville culture and that he was a valued member of his school community.

RETAINING BEST PRACTICES: RENEWING AND REORIENTING ■

Renewing

During the six years since Richard received tenure, he enjoyed many "renewing" experiences that were part of Centerville's commitment to retaining the successful members of their school community. As a member of the subcommittee on Building Block 5: Retaining, he helped develop and administer an annual survey of tenured faculty (Figure 5.3). They surveyed tenured faculty because they wanted to know the degree to which the respondents felt the district met their needs in the areas most likely to affect retention. Those needs included challenging work, important friendships, fair compensation, recognition, and opportunities for growth and development. As the results of the first survey indicated, there was a gap between what the district should be doing to retain staff and what the district was actually doing to retain staff. Centerville was losing tenured, successful staff members to other districts that offered more support, recognition, or compensation.

Figure 5.3   Survey of Tenured Educators: District Practices to Support Retention

DIRECTIONS: PLEASE CIRCLE ONE ANSWER IN EACH COLUMN FOR EACH ITEM: *1* IS THE LOWEST LEVEL OF IMPORTANCE *5* IS THE HIGHEST LEVEL OF IMPORTANCE **NS = NOT SURE**	COLUMN I *SHOULD BE* IMPORTANT TO THE DISTRICT?	COLUMN II *IS* IMPORTANT TO THE DISTRICT?
A. Your district is meeting your professional development needs successfully.	1 2 3 4 5 NS	1 2 3 4 5 NS
B. Your district recognizes you for your accomplishments.	1 2 3 4 5 NS	1 2 3 4 5 NS
C. Your district's purpose is to promote learning and safety so all students graduate.	1 2 3 4 5 NS	1 2 3 4 5 NS
D. Your district helps you develop and use professional practices that help students achieve learning and safety goals.	1 2 3 4 5 NS	1 2 3 4 5 NS
E. Your work is challenging for you.	1 2 3 4 5 NS	1 2 3 4 5 NS
F. Your work is rewarding for you.	1 2 3 4 5 NS	1 2 3 4 5 NS
G. You are provided with fair compensation for your work.	1 2 3 4 5 NS	1 2 3 4 5 NS
H. You are provided incentives to continue your professional growth and development.	1 2 3 4 5 NS	1 2 3 4 5 NS
I. The culture of the district makes you feel valued.	1 2 3 4 5 NS	1 2 3 4 5 NS
J. You have made friends in the district since you were hired.	1 2 3 4 5 NS	1 2 3 4 5 NS

DIRECTIONS: **PLEASE CIRCLE ONE ANSWER IN EACH COLUMN FOR EACH ITEM:** **1 IS THE LOWEST LEVEL OF IMPORTANCE** **5 IS THE HIGHEST LEVEL OF IMPORTANCE** **NS = NOT SURE**	**COLUMN I** **SHOULD BE** **IMPORTANT TO THE DISTRICT?**	**COLUMN II** **IS** **IMPORTANT TO THE DISTRICT?**
K. The program of supervision, observation, evaluation, and recognition helps you fulfill your role as a member of the district.	1 2 3 4 5 NS	1 2 3 4 5 NS
L. Your district makes you feel welcome.	1 2 3 4 5 NS	1 2 3 4 5 NS
M. Your building makes you feel welcome.	1 2 3 4 5 NS	1 2 3 4 5 NS

The Building Block 5 initiative helped Centerville close the gap, as was evident from successive surveys and other data. Tenured teachers were feeling more connected, motivated, and valued. More tenured, successful educators were remaining with Centerville, and Richard felt that the focus on renewing was a significant part of that success. He decided to illustrate "renewing" by presenting his "Top Eleven" (Figure 5.4) favorite experiences that helped him continue to feel as connected and motivated as he did during the first three years of his career in Centerville.

He discovered that these renewing experiences and the salary commitment increased his interest and willingness to participate in the reorienting process, which was the other best practice he wanted to feature in his presentation to the Induction Task Force.

Reorienting

Richard included two reorienting experiences to the Induction Task Force. The first experience was a minicourse in instructional delivery. The second was a new course focusing on co-teaching and inclusion.

Reorienting Experience #1: Minicourse on Instructional Delivery

As a Centerville teacher completing his fifth year since earning tenure, Richard was expected to complete a set number of hours in the district's

Figure 5.4 A Teacher's Top Eleven Favorite "Renewing" Experiences Since Receiving Tenure

1. Invited by the student body to lead the graduation procession.

2. Completed a series of courses paid for by the district.

3. Acknowledged at an end-of-year board of education meeting as "Educator of the Year" for his building.

4. Highlighted for three of his "best instructional practices" in the district professional journal and recognized in the local paper.

5. Presented the "Connecting Character to Conduct" character education award to a colleague at the Senior Awards Ceremony.

6. Relaxed by the commitment the board made to keep the salary schedule at the seventy-fifth percentile or better for their region of the state.

7. Offered an adult education course, Conversational Spanish.

8. Invited to co-present an overview of differentiating instruction at a recent faculty meeting.

9. Awarded a minigrant for integrating language instruction with career development and occupational studies.

10. Presented classroom management techniques at the New Educator Academy conducted during the summer.

11. Asked by students to advise the district's Faculty-Student Travel Club.

core curriculum for professional development. He chose a variety of programs, including a minicourse on instructional delivery. He was impressed by how new research helped him refine many of the practices he was using on a daily basis, as well as several practices that were new to him.[3] He wanted the Induction Task Force to understand that this part of the reorienting program made him feel

- More confident as a teacher
- More strongly connected to the district
- More strongly supported by the district

He also appreciated that the course was paid for by the district and conveniently located in a nearby learning center.

Reorienting Experience #2: Co-Teaching and Inclusion

During his eighth year of teaching, members of his department collaborated with members of the Special Education Department to pilot a co-taught, inclusion Spanish class for tenth-grade students. He and a special education teacher began their careers at Centerville together and volunteered to co-teach the new class.

As they explored the research regarding co-teaching and inclusion,[4] they felt that they needed to develop more strategies, activities, and materials to

- Help teachers work together successfully
- Help all their students learn the curriculum

At the same time, the Professional Development Committee was updating the core curriculum (Figure 3.3). The committee asked the staff for recommendations about how to improve the core curriculum so it was directly connected to federal and state mandates, district goals, assessments, updated standards of professional practice, and student needs. Two teachers suggested that the core curriculum include an introduction to co-teaching and inclusion. They further suggested that additional professional development activities should include a series of workshops, seminars, job-embedded professional development activities, and additions to the building-level professional libraries to help support the districtwide inclusion and co-teaching initiative.

Since many others agreed with the recommendation, the district added an "Introduction to Co-Teaching and Inclusion" course to the core curriculum. At the same time, all administrators participated in a "Leading for Learning"[5] workshop designed to help them observe, evaluate, and support Centerville's co-teaching and inclusion model.

He appreciated the concept of reorientation when he participated in the new core curriculum course in co-teaching and inclusion. For the first time since his early years as a teacher in Centerville, he felt some trepidation in his new role: co-teacher. He had never shared instructional time or space with anyone before on a regular basis, and neither had his special education colleague. She never taught so many students in one setting and was also concerned about her role in helping all the students learn the curriculum. They both felt slightly unsure of their individual and shared roles. After almost ten years of professional practice, they felt like novice teachers again, learning new skills to achieve new goals.

Once they completed the core curriculum course, they felt more confident. They were able to draw on their prior knowledge as well as the new things they researched and learned together. They quickly enrolled in the more intensive professional development activities that would support them as they became increasingly proficient as co-teachers and joined a team of teachers committed to researching how students were learning in response to new teacher practices.[6]

Richard closed this portion of his presentation to the Induction Task Force by making three basic points:

- That the Centerville professional culture promotes the notion that every teacher is a "new" teacher for his or her new students each year. As all the members of the school community grow and change, teachers and other educators need regular opportunities to literally "reorient" themselves to the evolving characteristics of the profession, the students, and the district.

- That change is a certainty for the school and for the community at large. Change would always be the most difficult aspect of the renewal and reorienting process. The requirements to complete reorienting activities gave all educators an opportunity to refine their skills.

- That the district continue to use Building Block 5: Retaining in the overall approach to attracting and retaining the right staff for the right reasons.

After summarizing these thoughts, Richard turned to his final talking point.

■ RETAINING BEST PRACTICE: GETTING TO THE "HEART" OF IT

"The core reason for Building Block 5 is to help the district retain the right educators for the right reasons. From my perspective as a teacher who has experienced all the building blocks, from recruitment to retention, I can identify why I and my colleagues continue to work here, despite the fact that educating children is hard work and we all face many challenges:

> First, I know what is expected of me.
> Second, I am welcome to contribute my expertise on a daily basis.
> Third, I feel supported here, even when I take risks and try new things.
> Fourth, I am recognized for my efforts and my accomplishments.
> Fifth, the people here matter to me, and I know I matter to them.
> Sixth, I feel that I am a visible, valued member of a productive team.
> Seventh, I love to teach, and this district helps me do my personal best every day."

As Richard concluded his presentation, he recalled a moment that best captured his commitment to remaining a member of the Centerville professional staff.

> In my second year, my principal observed a lesson where, to be charitable, everything went wrong. I thought my lesson plan was great. It just didn't work. Before the postobservation conference, I was beginning to doubt whether I was in the right profession, or if Centerville would even want to keep me. My principal did two things that made that meeting a defining moment in my professional life. First, he spent a few minutes commiserating with me . . . sharing with me that some of his lessons were not the perfect examples he wished they could have been. We even laughed when he confessed to checking the want ads in the beginning of his career, just to see if there was another career that might be better suited for him. He let me know that such experiences were part of all our "teacher lives."

But he did not stop by simply agreeing that some lessons are unsuccessful. He did not allow me to accept that poor lessons were inevitable. In fact, he said that the whole process of supervision, observation, and evaluation was basically a "we" thing: a system of supporting us so we can do a better job.

He reminded me that teacher practices are still the most important factors in helping our students learn. Then he asked how he could help me use some better practices. He made himself available, offered suggestions, and gave me the names of other colleagues who might be able to provide me with timely, sustained support. In that moment, I knew that I had a career in Centerville. I knew I was expected to try new things, ask for help, offer help, and that I could become a master teacher someday.

Richard concluded his presentation by stating, "My principal connected with me that day. In that moment, I connected with the district. And since that moment, I have been consciously making the same connections with my students and my colleagues. I want all my students to feel that I support them the way my supervisors support me: That our school succeeds because *we* support each other."

CHAPTER SUMMARY ■

It is becoming increasingly difficult for schools or districts to retain tenured or permanent educators. When experienced staff transfer to other schools or resign to go to other districts, they often say that they felt disconnected from the rest of their school community. These personnel losses create instability and increase the costs of both recruitment and professional development.

Many districts have a research-based program of observation and evaluation. They may even have a sophisticated professional development program based on data mining and careful assessment. They may still find those practices inadequate in retaining their best professional staff.

What is missing? The connection between the clinical practice of educating and the emotional intelligence of the school community as a whole. The "heart" of the matter is ensuring that good clinical practice resonates with emotional intelligence. This chapter was organized to demonstrate how a school or district can retain successful tenured/permanent educators through a supportive formal and informal mix of community activities, supervision, observation, professional development, and data mining. These clinical practices are more likely to produce their intended effects if they are implemented in the context of a school culture that values how each individual contributes equally and differently to the success of the entire school community. Our schools will either keep educators, or lose educators, one person at a time.

Tips

Connections

- The role of the Board of Education and Administration includes creating opportunities for all members of the school community to participate in meaningful professional development and other learning experiences that promote student learning and safety.
- Your district may maintain a faculty or community/school chorus, orchestra, theatre group, sports teams, clubs, etc…, which sustains and enriches connections between and among staff members.
- District or building level literary journal for faculty, staff, community, and students circulated through the district, posted on website, etc.
- Develop traditions for faculty, staff, parent, and community collaboration, such as doing the prom together.
- End-of-the-year or regular holiday-type barbecue, picnics joining school life with family life.
- After tenure/permanence, the teacher may use the portfolio to:
  - Reflect on professional growth and practices
  - As a form of documenting best practices he or she has used
  - To share with new and tenured colleagues

Data Mining

Regularly review and report data regarding:

- Retirements
- Newly hired educators
- Resignations
- Transfers
- Dual certifications
- Professional development programs and activities
- Percentage of teachers reaching new "benchmarks" in the salary or compensation schedule

Use the above data to:

- Make decisions regarding recruitment
- Make decisions regarding retention

Finance

Educators and other district personnel are compensated for participating in or facilitating professional development activities through:

- Negotiated stipends
- Inservice credit
- College and graduate credit
- Compliance with negotiated agreements requiring participation

(And **Professional Development**) Ensure that educators get time to participate in staff development by allocating sufficient resources, including

- Funds
- Time
- Materials
- Consultants and facilitators
- Administrative support for
  - Logistics
  - Implementing strategies taught in staff development

Legal Issues

- Develop and update policies and contracts to ensure that sufficient time and other resources are allocated for professional development.
- Keep in mind the federal, state and local laws, statutes, and policies when continuing your induction, supervision, observation, evaluation, promotion, and recognition of your staff.
- (And **Professional Development**) Regularly educate your entire staff regarding such issues as right to know/OSHA, sexual harassment, discrimination, universal precautions, and other such areas of importance.

Personnel Issues

- The role of the staff development person or office includes the following activities related to professional development: coordinating, scheduling, verifying, monitoring, assessing, refining, reporting.
- (And **Data Mining**) The Personnel Director uses appropriate software to maintain current professional development transcripts and portfolios for each educator.
- This process generates information important for individuals, schools, and the district to make decisions regarding contract compliance, professional development, and progress toward district and building goals.

Professional Development

- Inservice presentations are scheduled by the personnel director or a designee, such as another administrator, an administrative intern, an administrative secretary, the district clerk, a lead teacher, teacher center staff in collaboration with district administration, library/media specialist
- Bring job-embedded professional development to your school or district, so your educators can have real-time, on-site, during-the-school-day support in their efforts to apply the strategies, activities, and programs the district is expecting them to use. For example,
- Phase 1: The district hires the study skills expert to conduct two identical half-day workshops for social studies teachers of Grades 5–8. Twenty teachers are trained in the morning and twenty are trained in the afternoon. Ten substitutes are hired. Each one substitutes for two teachers, so the district gets maximum benefit and minimizes costs.
- Phase 2: The study skills expert offers the following on-site, during-the-day, job-embedded professional development:

- Model lessons using the study skills strategies and materials to help students achieve study skills goals
- Co-teaching using the study skills strategies and materials to help students achieve study skills goals
- Co-planning with the teachers who completed the study skills workshop
- Phase 3: Evaluation: Student performance is tested.

■ NOTES

1. Buckingham, M., & Coffman, C. (1999). *First break all the rules: What the world's greatest managers do differently.* New York: Simon & Schuster.

2. Deschenes, C., Ebeling, D., & Sprague, B. (2000). *Adapting curriculum and instruction in inclusive classrooms: A teacher's desk reference.* Bloomington: Center for School and Community Integration, The University-Affiliated Program of Indiana.

3. MacLean, M., & Mohr, M. (1999). *Teacher-researchers at work.* Berkeley, CA: National Writing Project.

4. Friend, M. (1999). *Including students with special needs: A practical guide for classroom teachers.* New York: Allyn & Bacon.

5. See Resource B for more information regarding "Leading for Learning and Safety."

6. MacLean & Mohr, 142-143.

BLUEPRINT FOR BUILDING BLOCK 5

Building Block 4	GOALS	PARTICIPANTS	OBJECTIVES	NEXT STEPS
_5a	**Keeping/Retaining Tenured/Permanent Staff**			
	• Retain professional staff beyond the year that permanent/tenure status is granted • Sustain connections among educators • Sustain connections between educators and district/schoolwide goals, programs, and practices • Reorientation and renewal	• Superintendent • Board of education • Administrators • Personnel director • Teacher Association members • Probationary teachers • Veteran teachers • Retirees • Consultants	• Data mine results of observations and annual professional performance reviews for trends, gaps, and overlaps • Data mine results of student assessments for trends, gaps, and overlaps • Survey staff • Involve staff in creating professional development programs and practices for faculty meetings, department meetings, etc. • Establish minimum hours for professional development for each educator each year • Regularly refine the reorientation/renewal program/practices • Implement a system of celebration for "We've Met Our Goals!"	• Celebrate • Evaluate • Reconvene the Centerville School District Task Force on Induction: Connecting Recruitment to Retention • Prepare the report to the superintendent and the board of education on the status of the districtwide induction program

(Continued)

BLUEPRINT FOR BUILDING BLOCK 5 *(Continued)*

	GOALS	PARTICIPANTS	OBJECTIVES	NEXT STEPS
__5b	Report to the board of education	• Superintendent • Personnel director • Optional: Other staff designated by the superintendent	Share qualitative and quantitative data regarding progress toward Connecting Recruitment to Retention initiative to achieve district learning and safety goals	Continuously refine, evaluate and report on the progress of the induction initiative

Endnote

We designed this book to help all the administrators, teachers, and board of education members who will be hiring the more than 2 million new teachers between now and 2015. Our goal was to support you through every aspect of the recruitment, induction, and retention process. As we noted in our introduction, recruiting educators is not just a matter of filling vacancies. It is a matter of shaping the future one professional, one child, one school community at a time.

As a composite of the many schools we've worked in over the past 35 years, Centerville symbolizes a school culture dedicated to promoting learning and safety through all their initiatives and practices, from curriculum development and assessment to recruitment and retention. In this book, we have provided a Blueprint you can use to help your district transform its culture by attracting and retaining the best professionals.

Now you have an opportunity to create your own Blueprint, capitalizing on the information in this book. From your Blueprint you can build what matters most in every district: not brick and mortar, but the human capital that will support your students now, and for years to come. Teachers often remain in a school or district for five, ten, sometimes thirty years and more. The investment you make in recruitment, induction, and retention—particularly in the early years—may be the most "profitable" investment your school district ever makes.

Resource A

BluePrint
for Building
Blocks 1–5

BLUEPRINT FOR BUILDING BLOCK 1

Building Block 1	GOALS	PARTICIPANTS	OBJECTIVES	NEXT STEPS
	Preparing			
__1a	Cabinet meeting on staffing	• Superintendent • Other lead administrators	Reach consensus regarding how to cope with the following issues in a way that is aligned with the district mission statement (see Figure 1.1). • Increasing numbers of retirements • Resignations of relatively new staff • New certifications needed to meet federal/state mandates and local goals/needs.	Superintendent presents to the board of education regarding the need for a more responsive induction policy
__1b	Board of Education: • Adopts a comprehensive induction policy • Incorporates the hiring policy into the induction policy • Sets a board goal regarding Induction: Connecting Recruitment to Retention	Board of Education Leadership Team: • Superintendent • Personnel Director	Superintendent and Cabinet begin to implement the induction policy	• Leadership Team implements district policy by adopting the Induction: Connecting Recruitment to Retention (I:CRR) approach • Members of the Leadership Team organize the district Induction Task Force

	GOALS	PARTICIPANTS	OBJECTIVES	NEXT STEPS
___1c	Induction Task Force convenes to create a framework matching Figure 1.2 [Induction Framewor]	• Superintendent • Board member • Personnel director • Building principals • Teachers Association • Chairpersons • Parent/community member	Establish (up to four) committees on Building Blocks of Induction: • Building Block 2: Staffing • Building Block 3: Orienting • Building Block 4: Connecting • Building Block 5: Retaining	Induction Task Force schedules workshops so all appropriate task force and other committee members learn the induction process
___1d	Workshops are convened	Members: • Induction Task Force Committee members	Two-day Induction: Connecting Recruitment to Retention workshop: • Topic 1: Team-Building • Topic 2: Using the Induction: Connecting Recruitment to Retention approach with BluePrint	• Evaluate the workshop process • Use the outcomes of the workshop evaluation to provide additional task force and committee training, as needed • Report progress to the superintendent
___1e	Establish a three-year induction plan to recruit and retain the best educators	Members: • Induction Task Force • Members of other committees	• Building Block committees use district data to draft a calendar for implementing "appropriate" elements of each Building Block (2 through 5) • Each committee creates a report to the Induction Task Force indicating status of each Building Block • Publicize outcomes, Building Block 1	Initiate all appropriate elements of each Building Block: 2-5

(Continued)

BLUEPRINT FOR BUILDING BLOCK 2

	GOALS	PARTICIPANTS	OBJECTIVES	NEXT STEPS
Building Block 2	**STAFFING: Recruiting Interviewing Hiring**			
_2a_	Staffing Committee convenes to: • Use BluePrint to make decisions • Identify objectives	Members should include representatives from: • Administration • Other educators • Parent/community	Establish subcommittees on: • Recruiting • Interviewing Assess need for training/development regarding staffing	Conduct training/development as needed Each subcommittee arranges: • Meeting dates • Activities consistent with the BluePrint
	Recruiting			
_2b_	Recruiting subcommittee convenes	Personnel director and others as appropriate	Gather and organize data regarding staffing needs over coming year(s)	• Use the staffing projections to prepare a recruitment plan that helps the district achieve its learning and safety goals • Monitor/assess/report progress
_2c_	Outreach subcommittee meets	• Personnel director • Members of the Recruitment Subcommittee	To reach out to nontraditional and traditional resources for educators consistent with staffing needs/goals	Coordinate outreach with advertising, public relations, and career ladder activities

	GOALS	PARTICIPANTS	OBJECTIVES	NEXT STEPS
_2d	Advertising subcommittee meets to set objectives	• Personnel director • Members of the Recruitment Subcommittee	To attract the best candidates to meet staffing needs/goals	Coordinate with outreach, public relations and career ladder activities
_2e	Public Relations subcommittee meets to set objectives	• Personnel director • Members of the Recruitment Subcommittee	To attract the best candidates to meet staffing needs/goals	Coordinate with outreach, public relations and career ladder activities
_2f	Career Ladder subcommittee meets to set objectives	• Personnel director • Members of the Recruitment Subcommittee	To attract the best candidates to meet staffing needs/goals	Coordinate with outreach, public relations and career ladder activities
_2g	Sustain the interviewing, hiring, and appointing process until all staffing needs are met.	• Personnel director • Other district and building/department/grade-level leaders • Interview tems	To recommend at least two equally qualified professional candidates for each available position	Use the data to make recommendations regarding the staffing initiative for the following year(s)
	Interviewing			
_2h	Interviewing subcommittee convenes to set objectives	Members	To complete training in I:CRR approach to interviewing	Plan the sequence of activities for: • Reviewing resumes • Interviewing • Evaluating demonstration lessons • Achieving consensus regarding making recommendations to move candidates forward toward hiring

(Continued)

113

BLUEPRINT FOR BUILDING BLOCK 2 *(Continued)*

	GOALS	PARTICIPANTS	OBJECTIVES	NEXT STEPS
__2i	Reviewing resumes	Members	Find best candidates for each position	Use data from resumes to select and schedule candidates
__2j	Using interview questioning techniques	Members	Evaluate candidates fairly on the same criteria	Use data from interview to select candidates for the demonstration lessons
__2k	Evaluating demonstration lessons	Members	Use standards of professional practice and criteria from the district's observation and evaluation program to evaluate demonstration lessons	• Use data from the demonstration lesson, interview, resume, etc., to advance selected candidates to the hiring phase • Prepare candidate's Review for Selection Packet
__2l	Interviewers send finalists to building, departmental, and/or central office interview stage	Could include: • Central office staff • Personnel director • Building principal • Department chair	Interviewers achieve consensus regarding recommendations to move candidates forward to the personnel director and superintendent	Superintendent follows district policy and board goals
	Hiring			
__2m	Superintendent recommends the most qualified candidates to the board of education	• Board of education • Superintendent • Personnel director	The board of education appoints the candidates that the superintendent recommends	Superintendent, personnel director, and others lead the district to take next steps toward retaining the newly recruited educators

BLUEPRINT FOR BUILDING BLOCK 3

	GOALS	PARTICIPANTS	OBJECTIVES	NEXT STEPS
Building Block 3	***Orienting***			
	Preorientation			
3a	• Develop procedures to help new educators "connect" with district/building/department/grades • Create core curriculum • Align supervision, observation, and evaluation with the core curriculum for new educators	• Personnel director • Building principals • Department chairs • Teacher Association • Other educators	Objectives: • Use data to develop **what** all new educators should know and do • Use data to decide **how** to implement a comprehensive induction program	Implement, monitor, assess, and refine the content and procedures that are part of "connecting" the new educator to the Centerville school community
3b	When new educators are hired, implement preorienting activities	• School/community leaders • Personnel director • Newly hired educators	The personnel director ensures that all newly hired educators receive necessary materials and schedules	Personnel director surveys the newly hired educators and others involved to evaluate the reaching out process

(Continued)

BLUEPRINT FOR BUILDING BLOCK 3 *(Continued)*

	GOALS	PARTICIPANTS	OBJECTIVES	NEXT STEPS
	Orientation			
_3c	Implement a districtwide orientation program	Key members of the district facilitate the orientation session	• Continue building and strengthening connections between and among members of the district • Provide opportunities for participants to earn credits or receive other kinds of compensation consistent with district policy • Help newly hired educators develop the shared language and goals of the Centerville school community	Personnel director uses the information, shares the results, and collaborates with other leaders to refine the orientation program
_3d	Implement building-level orientation programs	• Each newly hired educator • Building-level administrators • Lead teachers • Districtwide staff, when appropriate, including pupil personnel and department chairs • Personnel director	Formal: • Principal/AP invites newly hired educators to specific programs Informal: • New/veteran staff meet, share ideas; newly hired educator reports to the office and visits; may set up classroom for the year • Strengthen connections, make newly hired educators and veterans feel welcome and secure	• Sustain culture of collaboration and mutual support • Create formal, schedule-based opportunities for staff members to collaborate

	GOALS	PARTICIPANTS	OBJECTIVES	NEXT STEPS
	Professional Development			
_3e	Conduct monthly districtwide professional development programs for newly hired educators	• All newly hired educators • Administrators • Department chairs • Lead teachers • Consultants	• Ensure that professional development programs advance the learning and safety goals of the district • Choose professional development subjects on the basis of ongoing data mining	• Create, monitor, and assess impact of the professional development plan (PDP) of each new educator • Establish mentor-mentee relationships based on data indicating strengths and needs of each
_3f	Use data to plan and implement end of school year	All probationary educators	Ensure that topics of the professional development programs advance the learning and safety goals of the district	Refine, evaluate, and report on progress of professional development
	Mentoring/Collaborating			
_3g	Research mentoring models	• Administrators • Teachers • University staff • Consultants	Propose one or more mentoring and collaboration models so each new teacher is formally connected with at least one other educator who can fulfill the role of mentor during at least one academic year	Ensure mentoring models are appropriately differentiated to meet district, student, and staff needs

(Continued)

117

BLUEPRINT FOR BUILDING BLOCK 3 (Continued)

	GOALS	PARTICIPANTS	OBJECTIVES	NEXT STEPS
__3h	Implement and sustain the mentoring practices	• Mentors-mentees • Building administrators • Teacher Association leaders	Connect newly hired educators with tenured/permanent members of the staff	Regularly evaluate progress and adjust accordingly
	Supervising, Observing, and Evaluating			
__3i	Develop a program that helps the district: • Meet learning and safety goals • Attract and retain the best educators for the district • Ensure use of best practices	• Administrators • Teacher Association members • Veteran teachers • Department chairs • Newly tenured teachers • Newly hired educators • Retirees • Consultants	Pilot the program	• Evaluate the program • Evaluate the individual practices of the staff members involved • Make appropriate staffing decisions • Make appropriate changes in the program
__3j	Implement the districtwide program of supervision, observation, and evaluation	• All probationary educators • Administrators • Department chairs • Lead teachers • Consultants	• Conduct at least four formal evaluations per probationary year • Evaluate educator performance in regard to district/ building-level goals	Use the data to: • Establish professional development topics and goals for the end-of-school-year Probationary Educators' Workshops • Identify newly hired educators in need of additional support • Provide appropriate support • Evaluate progress • Make appropriate staffing decisions

BLUEPRINT FOR BUILDING BLOCK 4

Building Block 4	GOALS	PARTICIPANTS	OBJECTIVES	NEXT STEPS
	Connecting	**For the Probationary Educators' Second and Third Year**		
	Professional Development			
__4a	Ongoing professional development • Formal: 15 hours • Approved by the principal/supervisor	All probationary second- and third-year teachers • Total of 30 hours of formal professional development	• Train and retain the best educators for Centerville School District • Implement an approach to professional development that celebrates the strengths of the staff as professional development trainers who work collaboratively with probationary educators • Nurture new educators through ongoing professional development	Help newly hired educators use best practices associated with helping all students achieve academic and safety goals

(Continued)

BLUEPRINT FOR BUILDING BLOCK 4 *(Continued)*

	GOALS	PARTICIPANTS	OBJECTIVES		NEXT STEPS
	Supervising, Observing, and Evaluating				
__4b	Developing lasting connections with administrators, colleagues, and students through formal as well as informal supervision, observation, and evaluation	Principal, curriculum supervisors, probationary teachers	• Develop a "team" culture of supervision, observation, and evaluation to celebrate best practices for supervising, teaching, and learning • Use formal and informal observation to connect probationary staff with others in the effort to meet/exceed benchmarks established by the district and state		• Continue to develop/celebrate best teaching practices that reflect the district's standards of professional practice • Data mine the impact of observation/supervision/ evaluation of best teaching practices on student achievement
	Granting Tenure/ Permanence				
__4c	Superintendent recommends to the board of education that the identified probationary educators be granted permanent status/tenure	• Superintendent • Board of education • Administrators • Probationary teachers	• Retaining the best educators for Centerville School District • Implement a tenure celebration tradition • Continue to nurture newly permanent/tenured educators		Help newly permanent, tenured educators consistently use standards of professional practice to make decisions and select practices

BLUEPRINT FOR BUILDING BLOCK 5

Building Block 4	GOALS	PARTICIPANTS	OBJECTIVES	NEXT STEPS
	Keeping/Retaining Tenured/Permanent Staff			
__ **5a**	• Retain professional staff beyond the year that permanent/tenure status is granted • Sustain connections among educators • Sustain connections between educators and district/schoolwide goals, programs, and practices • Reorientation and renewal	• Superintendent • Board of education • Administrators • Personnel director • Teacher Association members • Probationary teachers • Veteran teachers • Retirees • Consultants	• Data mine results of observations and annual professional performance reviews for trends, gaps, and overlaps • Data mine results of student assessments for trends, gaps, and overlaps • Survey staff • Involve staff in creating professional development programs and practices for faculty meetings, department meetings, etc. • Establish minimum hours for professional development for each educator each year • Regularly refine the reorientation/renewal program/practices • Implement a system of celebration for "We've Met Our Goals!"	• Celebrate • Evaluate • Reconvene the Centerville School District Task Force on Induction: Connecting Recruitment to Retention • Prepare the report to the superintendent and the board of education on the status of the districtwide induction program

(Continued)

121

BLUEPRINT FOR BUILDING BLOCK 5 (Continued)

	GOALS	PARTICIPANTS	OBJECTIVES	NEXT STEPS
_5b	Report to the board of education	• Superintendent • Personnel director • Optional: Other staff designated by the superintendent	Share qualitative and quantitative data regarding progress toward Connecting Recruitment to Retention initiative to achieve district learning and safety goals	Continuously refine, evaluate and report on the progress of the induction initiative

Resource B

LEADING FOR LEARNING AND SAFETY

A Leadership Development Institute

Goal	*This institute is organized to help school leaders make decisions and take systemic, daily actions that measurably advance student learning, safety, and graduation.*
	This goal applies whether schools are implementing an innovation or simply updating skills and focus.
	This leadership module is entirely customized to meet district or building priorities. *It can focus on decisions regarding such issues as recruitment, professional development, retention, curriculum instruction, assessment, parent involvement, building maintenance, transportation, athletics, or any other area of school leadership important to the district or building.*
Participants	*Can include but need not be limited to:*
	• *Board of education members*
	• *District administrators*
	• *Building administrators*
	• *Lead teachers*
	• *Other district, building, parent, and community leaders*
Facilitators	*Members of the consulting team that developed the **Connecting Character to Conduct** approach and the **Induction: Connecting Recruitment to Retention** approach*
Key Topics	• *Achieving consensus on shared purpose, roles, and rules*
	• *Mapping the daily opportunities to promote learning, safety, and graduation through daily activities from monitoring halls to observing classes, designing advanced placement courses, or organizing field trips*
Format	• *Workshop*
	• *Job-embedded professional development*
Evaluation	*Data mining in areas of interest to the district such as:*
	• *Induction/recruitment and retention*
	• *Student conduct*
	• *Student academic performance*
	• *Parent involvement*
	• *Graduation rates, etc.*
Ongoing Support	• *As determined through the consensus of the participants.*

SOURCE: Richin, R., Banyon, R., Stein, R., Banyon, F. (2000). *Leading for Learning and Safety* (Training Module). Stony Brook, New York: Connecting Character to Conduct.

Resource C

AFFIRM, NORMALIZE, AND REFOCUS

A Three-Step Consensus-Building, Conflict-Reducing, Communication Strategy

Principle	People of all ages are more likely to listen to us carefully and work to find common ground with us if we demonstrate that we: (a) Listen to them carefully and (b) Establish some common ground with them by agreeing to even very small things.		
Process	While sustaining appropriate eye contact and other appropriate body language . . .		
Step 1: Affirm	*Find* where you can honestly *agree* with even one small element of something that someone has said, even if you disagree with most of it.	*Ex:*	In a meeting where the mentor's goal is to help the new teacher use motivating strategies and activities, a new teacher says to the mentor, "The kids just weren't motivated to learn today." Mentor AFFIRMS by replying, "You're right . . . <u>our students are often not motivated to learn the material we are teaching.</u>"

Step 2: Normalize	*Acknowledge* that there may be many other people who feel the same way.	*Ex:*	Mentor NORMALIZES by continuing, "All teachers have that experience at one point or another…"
Step 3: Refocus	*Connect* the point where you agreed (in Step 1) to the goal you were pursuing with the individual or group.	*Ex:*	Mentor REFOCUSES the conversation onto the goal by saying, "So we need to discover ways to help students feel motivated through our strategies and activities, if not through the content itself. For example, we know that middle school students are motivated to talk and express their opinions. So you can help them feel more motivated by explaining how the cooperative learning activity will give everyone an opportunity to critique the project."

SOURCE: Richin, R., Banyon, R., Stein, R., Banyon, F. (2000). *Leading for Learning and Safety* (Training Module). Stony Brook, NY: Connecting Character to Conduct.

Resource D

PARTICULARS OF THE LETTER OF INTENT/BINDER

CENTERVILLE SCHOOL DISTRICT

Date: _____

NOTICE OF TEACHER APPOINTMENT AND ACCEPTANCE

Subject to approval by the Superintendent of Schools and the Board of Education, the following appointment has been made:

NAME: _____

ASSIGNMENT: _____

EFFECTIVE DATE(S):_____

PROBATIONARY: _____

AREA: _____

STEP AND SCHEDULE: STARTING SALARY:

_____   _____

PERSONNEL ADMINISTRATOR   ASSISTANT SUPERINTENDENT

_____   _____

TEACHER ACCEPTING   SUPERINTENDENT OF SCHOOLS
APPOINTMENT

Note: Starting salary, step, and schedule placement are based on data presented by the candidate at the time of hiring. This information must be documented by the candidate. Salary placement is not negotiable at a future date.

    All references will be checked prior to the presentation of the candidate's credentials to the Superintendent of Schools and the Board of Education. Any negative references will preclude this presentation.

Resource E

LETTER OF APPOINTMENT

CENTERVILLE SCHOOL DISTRICT

September 20, 200X

Dear _____

I am delighted to inform you that at the Board of Education meeting of _____, I recommended the approval of your probationary appointment to the position of elementary teacher.

We are pleased to have you with us and we wish you the very best as a member of our teaching staff.

Please indicate your acceptance of this appointment by signing the copy of this letter and returning it to Stephanie Blair, Centerville School District Personnel Director.

Sincerely,

Dr. James Frasier
Superintendent of Schools
cc: S. Blair

Assignment: _____

Effective Date: _____

Tenure Area: _____

Probationary Period: _____

Salary Step/Column: _____

_____   _____

(Date)   (Signature)

Resource F

ADVERTISEMENT FOR STAFFING POSITIONS

Centerville School District

"Dedicated to helping all children learn well and stay safe."

WE ANTICIPATE THE FOLLOWING VACANCIES

FOR THE 1999 – 2000 SCHOOL YEAR

❑ **Elementary teachers with dual certification in either reading/mathematics/special education/or English to speakers of other languages (ESOL)**

❑ **Secondary teachers (Grades 7-12)**
   o   English Language Arts
   o   Social Studies
   o   Mathematics
   o   Science - Dual certification in at least two of the following areas:
      ▪ Earth Science/Chemistry/Physics/Biology/General Science
   o   Languages other than English

❑ **K-12**
   o   Special Education
   o   Health and Physical Education (dual certified)
   o   Arts: Fine and Performing
   o   Technology Education
   o   Computer Education
   o   Home and Career
   o   Pupil Personnel: Social Worker, Guidance Counselor, and Psychologist

Join Our Centerville Team!

All interested candidates must submit the following items POSTMARKED BY March 1, 1999 to:

Ms. Stephanie Blair, Personnel Director, Centerville School District, 111 Centerville Street, Centerville, USA 11111-1111 or email at sblair@centerville.edu:
   ▪ Cover letter, including name, phone, address, position sought
   ▪ Resume not to exceed two pages
   ▪ Copy of transcripts and certification(s)
   ▪ Self-addressed, stamped postcard to acknowledge receipt

Centerville School District is committed to promoting a diverse workforce.

Resource G

TENURE LETTER

Centerville School District
Centerville, U.S.A.
Fax: 222-222-2222
Email: centerville@csd.k12.us

May 14, 200X
Ms. Irina Henshaw
211 East Main Street
Centerville, U.S.A.

Dear Irina:

As you know, the Board of Education at its meeting of May 13, 200X, acted to grant you tenure as an elementary school teacher (Grade 2) effective September 1, 200X. The public commendations, which were expressed by the Board, reflect the confidence all of us have in you as a committed educator.

I extend my personal good wishes to you for a long and enriching association with the Centerville schools. Thank you for your dedicated and caring service to the Centerville students.

Very truly yours,

Dr. Simon Frasier
Superintendent
F/lt

Resource H

EXEMPLAR FOR HOW TO USE AN EVALUATION INSTRUMENT (SEE RESOURCE I) IN THE PREOBSERVATION, OBSERVATION, AND POSTOBSERVATION

Schools have transformed educator practices by using the nine standards of professional practice as the basis for all phases of evaluating professional performance.

Preobservation Conference:

Time required: Approximately 20 minutes

The process begins with an appointment between the administrator and the teacher. The initial appointment is designed for what we refer to as a "preobservation conference." It is the practice of the observer to send the teacher a note the week before formally observing the teacher.

During the preobservation conference, the teacher brings:

- Lesson plans
- Additional material pertaining to the state standards related to the lesson
- Learning objectives the students will achieve during the lesson
- Teacher strategies and student activities
- Assessment strategies and materials

During the preobservation conference, the observer brings:

- A copy of the evaluation instrument so the teacher can see the focus of the criteria for evaluation
- Any recent, prior observations that included recommendations

The observer may ask how the teacher plans to respond to the recommendations in his or her lesson.

At Centerville, both the observer and the teacher agree on the general focus of the formal observation. The model is based on mutual trust. The purpose of the supervision/observation program is to enhance achievement and safety for all students by improving instructional delivery and classroom management.

The preobservation conference ends when both participants feel confident that the other understands the goals and procedures of the lesson and that the lesson meets the criteria of the district. At the conclusion of the meeting each one knows what will take place when the formal observation happens.

Observation:

Time Required: Approximately 40 minutes

The observer records observations on the template the district uses for this purpose.

The Postobservation Conference

Time Required: Flexible

Shortly after the observation, the observer and teacher meet. During this conference, they review the teacher's performance in the context of the nine standards of professional practice (Figure 2.6). They also focus on how the teacher helped the students achieve the intended objective.

As a result of the observation, Mr. Smith found that the teacher:

- Accommodated the needs of her students in her instructional delivery and materials development
- Developed a lesson to address different student needs

Centerville School District Observation Template

Standards of Professional Practice	Indicators of Presence or Absence of Standards of Professional Practice
Content Area(s) and Standards	Very knowledgeable of Hinduism and related the learning standards
Instructional Delivery	The teacher: • Began lesson with a "Do Now" activity engaging all students in using document based questions • Used a variety of modalities, such as overhead projector and computer, to focus learners • Transitioned smoothly to stating the objective and involving students in comparing and contrasting elements of the class and caste system of the United States and India, respectively
Classroom Management and Supervision	The teacher: • Responds to students with positive feedback, sustained questions, and involves students in projecting their voices and directing their comments to class at large • Asks students to listen to and respond respectfully to each other's questions and comments • Connects instructional delivery and classroom management seamlessly
Knowledge of Student Characteristics and Needs	• Teacher varied use of input, output, time, and level of support to ensure that all students learned • Teacher adhered to requirements of the IEP of identified students in regard to Hinduism and specifically differentiated instruction for students with severe disabilities (use of assistive technology for student with hearing disability)
Planning and Preparation	The written lesson plan included: • Standards, key ideas, performance indicators, and learner objectives • Evidence of preparation in the documents and worksheets she produced for the students • Adaptation to meet the needs of the students
Collaboration	The teacher: • Collaborated with the instructor of the differentiated instruction course, who was the instructor for the inservice course • Collaborated with the district technology resource and librarian to use technology appropriately

(Continued)

Centerville School District Observation Template (Continued)

Reflective and Responsive Practices	• In our preobservation conference we focused on differentiated instruction • During the lesson, the teacher addressed key points raised in the preobservation conference
Evaluation/ Assessment of Student Learning	The teacher: • Checked for student understanding, monitored and assessed student progress, allowed for different rate/pace of learning, and used a three-minute quiz to involve students in immediately recalling key points of the lesson • Used closure appropriately • Assigned "practice" (the Centerville term for homework) and gave students an estimated time frame in which they should complete the homework
Professional Responsibilities	The teacher: • Received the recommendations of the assistant principal appropriately • Expressed interest in continuing her professional development and thanked her supervisor for allowing her to take a risk by using a very new instructional strategy during a formal observation • Accepted constructive corrections appropriately

- Varied homework assignments based on student needs
- Used different instructional strategies such as whole group, cooperative and individualized instruction
- Successfully met the teacher's objectives

The observer suggested that the teacher enroll in additional courses on differentiating instruction, especially with the use of technology.

They conclude by agreeing that the lesson was satisfactory and that the teacher was using best practices to help her students learn well and stay safe.

Resource I

EVALUATION INSTRUMENT

Based on Half Hollow Hills School District 2000–2002 Standards of Professional Practice

It is recommended that:

A. All forms and processes for supervision, observation, and evaluation:
- Be based on state or other accepted standards of professional practice
- Be collaboratively constructed and consistently applied across and within the district

B. All those responsible for conducting supervision, observation and evaluation should complete specific training to ensure that the instrument is used consistently and correctly

C. All staff members who will be supervised, observed, and evaluated on the basis of the instrument should complete inservice training to help them use the district evaluation process as part of their own professional growth

This sample was developed with substantive input from administrators, teachers, and other educators. The Half Hollow Hills School District uses this instrument as the organizing framework for preobservations, observations, postobservations, and summative evaluations.

Standards of Professional Practice	*Sample Indicators of Professional Practice*
Content Area(s) and Standards	(a) *Demonstrates thorough knowledge of the subject matter* (b) *Demonstrates thorough knowledge of the curriculum*
Instructional Delivery	(a) *Demonstrates delivery of instruction that results in active student involvement* (b) *Develops a variety of questioning strategies to assess specific objectives*
Classroom Management and Supervision	(a) *Demonstrates classroom management skills that create an environment conducive to student learning* (b) *Demonstrates classroom management skills supporting diverse student learning needs; adjusts the pace of lessons and utilizes wait time appropriately*
Knowledge of Student Characteristics and Needs	(a) *Demonstrates knowledge of student development for the benefit of all students* (b) *Applies developmentally appropriate instructional strategies for the benefit of all students*
Planning and Preparation	(a) *Develops a comprehensive plan for instruction employing necessary pedagogical practices* (b) *Sets curriculum goals and learning expectations*
Collaboration	*Develops:* (a) *effective collaborative relationships with students to meet their learning needs* (b) *effective collaborative relationships with parents and colleagues*
Reflective and Responsive Practices	(a) *Reviews and assesses teaching practices on a regular basis* (b) *Attends appropriate conferences, workshops, and other professional development activities*
Evaluation/ Assessment of Student Learning	(a) *Implements assessment techniques based on appropriate learning standards designed to measure student progress* (b) *Communicates student progress to parents*
Professional Responsibilities	(a) *Handles professional obligations in an efficient, effective manner* (b) *Participates in school/district/community activities and committees*

Evaluation Grid			
	Satisfactory	*Needs Improvement*	*Unsatisfactory*
Content area(s) and standards			
Classroom management and supervision			
Knowledge of student characteristics and needs			
Planning and preparation			
Collaboration			
Reflective and responsive practices			
Evaluation/assessment of student learning			
Professional responsibilities			

Overall Rating: □ Satisfactory □ Needs Improvement □ Unsatisfactory
Narrative on opposite side of this evaluation form: See sample narrative on following page:

Teacher's signature:

_____

Observer's signature:

_____

Date:

_____

Recommendations for completing professional development activities:

Suggestions for conducting professional development activities:

Resource J

ORGANIZATIONAL CHART OF THE INDUCTION TASK FORCE

Organizational Chart of the Task Force

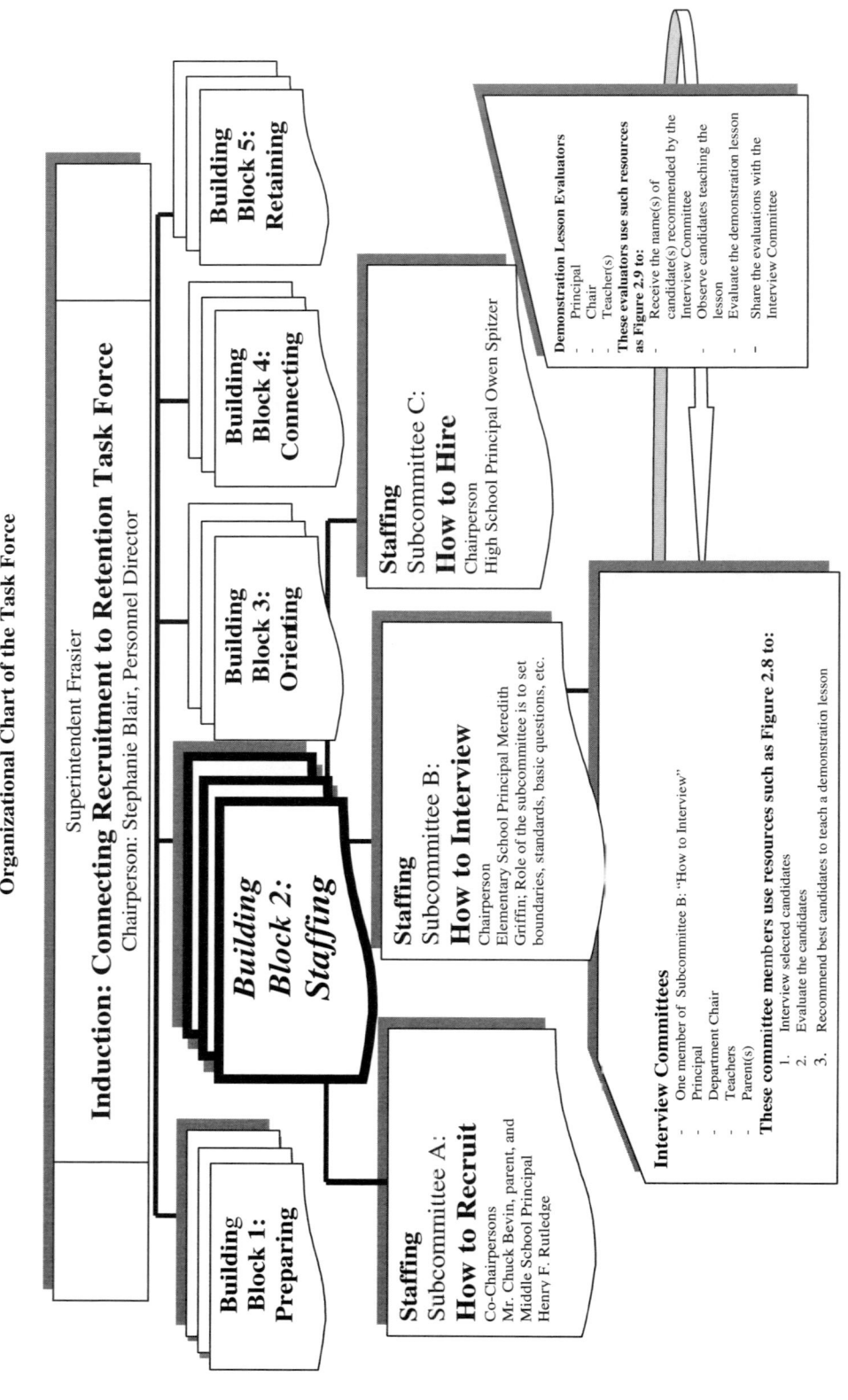

Superintendent Frasier

Induction: Connecting Recruitment to Retention Task Force

Chairperson: Stephanie Blair, Personnel Director

Building Block 1: Preparing

Building Block 2: Staffing

Building Block 3: Orienting

Building Block 4: Connecting

Building Block 5: Retaining

Staffing Subcommittee A: How to Recruit

Co-Chairpersons
Mr. Chuck Bevin, parent, and
Middle School Principal
Henry F. Rutledge

Staffing Subcommittee B: How to Interview

Chairperson
Elementary School Principal Meredith
Griffin; Role of the subcommittee is to set
boundaries, standards, basic questions, etc.

Staffing Subcommittee C: How to Hire

Chairperson
High School Principal Owen Spitzer

Interview Committees

-   One member of Subcommittee B: "How to Interview"
-   Principal
-   Department Chair
-   Teachers
-   Parent(s)

These committee members use resources such as Figure 2.8 to:

1.   Interview selected candidates
2.   Evaluate the candidates
3.   Recommend best candidates to teach a demonstration lesson

Demonstration Lesson Evaluators

-   Principal
-   Chair
-   Teacher(s)

These evaluators use such resources as Figure 2.9 to:

-   Receive the name(s) of candidate(s) recommended by the Interview Committee
-   Observe candidates teaching the lesson
-   Evaluate the demonstration lesson
-   Share the evaluations with the Interview Committee

Bibliography

Adler, M. (1982). *The Paideia proposal*. New York: Macmillan.

Anderson, G., Herr, K., & Nihlen, A. (1994). *Studying your own school*. Thousand Oaks, CA: Corwin.

Association of American University Presses Task Force on Bias-Free Language. (1995). *Guidelines for bias-free writing*. Bloomington: Indiana University Press.

Atkins, A. (1991). A sensible, faculty-designed model for curriculum development. *Journal of Curriculum and Supervision, 6,* 312-24.

Bacall, A. (2002). *The lighter side of educational leadership*. Thousand Oaks, CA: Corwin.

Barth, R. (1990). *Improving schools from within*. San Francisco: Jossey-Bass.

Buckingham, M. & Coffman, C. (1999). *First break all the rules: What the world's greatest managers do differently*. New York: Simon & Schuster.

Campbell, C. & Dahir, C. (1997). *The national standards for school counseling*. Alexandria, VA: American School Counselor Association.

Carew, D., Parisi-Carew, E. & Johnson, S. (2001). *High five: The magic of working together*. New York: HarperCollins.

Carnegie Council on Adolescent Development, Task Force on Education of Young Adolescents. (2000). *Turning points: Educating adolescents in the 21ˢᵗ century*. Washington, DC: Carnegie Council on Adolescent Development.

Carver, J. (1997). *Boards that make a difference: A new design for leadership in nonprofit and public organizations*. San Francisco: Jossey-Bass.

Cattani, D. (2002). *A classroom of her own: How new teachers develop instructional, professional and cultural competence*. Thousand Oaks, CA: Corwin.

Chase, B. (1998). The NEA's role: Cultivating teacher professionalism. *Educational Leadership, 55*(5), 18-20.

Cohen, N. (1995). *Mentoring adult learners*. Malabar, FL: Krieger.

Collay, M. et al. (1998). *Learning circles: Creating conditions for professional development*. Thousand Oaks, CA: Corwin.

Cooper, I. & Tomlinson, K. (2002). *Breaking through the glass ceiling: Recognizing the achievements of women in the 20ᵗʰ century*. Hauppauge, NY: Suffolk Academy of Law/Nassau Academy of Law.

Csikszentmihaly, M. (1997). *Finding flow: The psychology of engagement with everyday life*. NY: Basic Books.

Daloz, L. (1999). *Mentor: Guiding the journey of adult learners.* San Francisco: Jossey-Bass.

Darling-Hammond, L. (1997). *Doing what matters most: Investing in quality teaching.* New York: National Commission on Teaching and America's Future.

Darling-Hammond, L. (1998). Teacher learning that supports student learning. *Educational Leadership, 55*(5).

Darling-Hammond, L. (2000). *Solving the dilemmas of teacher supply, demand and standards.* New York: National Commission on Teaching and America's Future.

Darling-Hammond, L. (2001). *The research and the rhetoric on teacher certification.* New York: National Commission on Teaching and America's Future.

Deschenes, C., Ebeling, D. & Sprague, J. (2000). *Adapting curriculum and instruction in inclusive classrooms.* Bloomington: Center for School and Community Integration: The University-Affiliated Program of Indiana.

Diez, M. & Blackwell, P. (2001). *Quality assessment for quality outcomes.* Washington, DC: National Council for Accreditation of Teacher Education.

Dyson, A. (1997). *What difference does difference make? Teacher reflections on diversity, literacy and the urban primary school.* Urbana, IL: National Council of Teachers of English.

Educational Testing Service. (2000). *How teaching matters: Bringing the classroom back to discussions of teacher quality.* Princeton, NJ: Author.

Fideler, E. (2000). State initiative induction programs: Support, assisting, training, assessing and keeping teachers. *NASBE State Education Standard, 1*(1), 12-16.

Friend, M. (1999). *Including students with special needs: A practical guide for classroom teachers.* New York: Allyn & Bacon.

Gallos, J. & Ramsey, V. (1996). *Teaching diversity: Listening to the soul, speaking from the heart.* New York: Jossey-Bass Higher and Adult Education Series.

Gardner, H. (2000). *The disciplined mind.* New York: Penguin.

Glick, C. (2002). *Leadership for learning: How to help teachers succeed.* Alexandria, VA: ASCD.

Glickman, C. (1990). *Supervision of instruction.* Boston: Allyn & Bacon.

Goldberg, M. (2001). *Lessons from exceptional school leaders.* Alexandria, VA: ASCD.

Goldberg, M. (2001). Leadership in education: Five commonalities. *Phi Delta Kappan, 82*(10), 757-61.

Good, T. & Brophy, J. (1994). *Looking in classrooms.* New York: HarperCollins.

King, J., Hollins, E., & Hayman, W. (Eds.). (1997). *Preparing teachers for cultural diversity.* New York: Teachers College Press.

Kuzmeskus, J. (Ed.). (1996). *We teach them all: Teachers writing about diversity.* York, ME: Stenhouse.

MacLean, M. & Mohr, M. (1999). *Teacher-researchers at work.* Berkeley, CA: National Writing Project.

Nadeau, A. (Project Director), Leighton, M. (Writer). (1996, July). *The role of leadership in sustaining school reform: Voices from the field.* Washington, DC: U.S. Department of Education.

National Staff Development Council. (2001). *E-learning for professional development.* Oxford, OH: Author.

National Staff Development Council. (2001). *National Staff Development Council standards for staff development.* Oxford, OH: Author.

Norlander-Case, K., Reagan, T., Case, C. (1999, June). *The professional teacher, Vol. 4. The preparation and nurturance of the reflective practitioner.* San Francisco: Jossey-Bass.

Olson, L. (2002, June 12). Schools discovering riches in data. *Education Week.*

Perez, K., Swain, C., & Hartsough, C. (1997, Spring). An analysis of practices used to support new teachers. *Teacher Education Quarterly,* 41-52.

Podsen, I. & Denmark, V. (2000). *Coaching and mentoring first-year and student teachers.* New York: Eye on Education.

Portner, H. (1998). *Mentoring new teachers.* Thousand Oaks, CA: Corwin.

Ramsey, C. (1997). *A guide to supervision, observation and evaluation.* Centereach, New York: Middle Country Central School District.

Renyi, J. (1996). *Teachers taking charge of their own learning: Transforming professional development for student success.* Washington, DC: National Education Association for the Improvement of Education.

Schmidt, J. (1999). *Counseling in schools: Essential services and comprehensive programs.* Boston: Allyn & Bacon.

Sergiovanni, T. (1994). *Building community in schools.* San Francisco: Jossey-Bass.

Stein, R., Richin, R., Banyon, R. Banyon, F., & Stein, M. (2000). *Connecting character to conduct: Helping students do the right things.* Alexandria, VA: ASCD.

Stein, R., Richin, R., Banyon, R., & Banyon, F. (2000). *The first ten days of school: A desk manual for administrators, teachers and pupil personnel.* New York: CCC.

Toledo Federation of Teachers. (1998). *The Toledo Plan.* Retrieved July 15, 2002, from www.tft250.org/peer_review.htm.

Vella, J. (1995). *Training through dialogue: Promoting effective learning and change with adults.* San Francisco: Jossey-Bass.

Villani, S. (2002). *Mentoring programs for new teachers.* Thousand Oaks, CA: Corwin.

Weiss, E. & Weiss, S. (1999). Beginning teacher induction. *ERIC Digest.* ED 436487.

Wong, H. & Wong, R. (1998). *The first days of school.* Mountainview, CA: Harry Wong.

Index

CORWIN PRESS

The Corwin Press logo—a raven striding across an open book—represents the happy union of courage and learning. We are a professional-level publisher of books and journals for K-12 educators, and we are committed to creating and providing resources that embody these qualities. Corwin's motto is "Success for All Learners."